CW01430974

WITTGENSTEIN'S PRIVATE LANGUAGE

WITTGENSTEIN'S PRIVATE LANGUAGE

Grammar, Nonsense, and Imagination in
Philosophical Investigations, *§§243–315*

STEPHEN MULHALL

CLARENDON PRESS · OXFORD

OXFORD
UNIVERSITY PRESS

Great Clarendon Street, Oxford OX2 6DP

Oxford University Press is a department of the University of Oxford.
It furthers the University's objective of excellence in research, scholarship,
and education by publishing worldwide in

Oxford New York

Auckland Cape Town Dar es Salaam Hong Kong Karachi
Kuala Lumpur Madrid Melbourne Mexico City Nairobi
New Delhi Shanghai Taipei Toronto

With offices in

Argentina Austria Brazil Chile Czech Republic France Greece
Guatemala Hungary Italy Japan Poland Portugal Singapore
South Korea Switzerland Thailand Turkey Ukraine Vietnam

Oxford is a registered trademark of Oxford University Press
in the UK and in certain other countries

Published in the United States
by Oxford University Press Inc., New York

British Library Cataloguing in Publication Data

Data available

Library of Congress Cataloging in Publication Data

Data available

Typeset by Laserwords Private Limited, Chennai, India
Printed in Great Britain
on acid-free paper by
Biddles Ltd., King's Lynn, Norfolk

ISBN 0–19–920854–9   978–0–19–920854–8

1 3 5 7 9 10 8 6 4 2

If language represents our ineluctable publicness, then language as free association is the closest we can get to speaking that contradiction in terms, a private language, a language of desire.

Adam Phillips

Contents

Acknowledgements

The author and publisher would like to thank Blackwell Publishers for kind permission to reproduce material from the *Philosophical Investigations* (2nd Edition), by Ludwig Wittgenstein.

The author would also like to acknowledge the very useful comments of two anonymous readers of the manuscript for Oxford University Press, and the forbearance of Alison, Matthew and Eleanor during its composition.

Introduction: Wittgenstein's Aesthetics of Austerity

Although my primary concern in this essay is with Wittgenstein's *Philosophical Investigations*,[1] and specifically with its famous sequence of remarks on the idea of a private language, my approach to those remarks takes its orientation from a set of issues that have dominated a rather different corner of the field of Wittgenstein studies for the last decade. The corner is that relating to the *Tractatus Logico-Philosophicus*;[2] and the issues concern the philosophical method employed in that book—a method which engenders its notorious concluding declaration that anyone who understands its author must recognize that the elucidatory propositions that make it up (propositions that appear to express a variety of substantial views about the essence of language, thought, and world, and that must presumably provide whatever grounds there are for this conclusion itself) are nonsensical.

Plainly, a great deal hangs on how one understands the notion of 'nonsense' in the context of this declaration, and so of the book as a whole; and much recent discussion of the matter has focused on the relative merits of two ways of doing this.[3] One way is to invoke what has been called a substantial conception of nonsense. This approach would have it that the propositions of the *Tractatus* exemplify a kind of nonsense that is distinct

[1] Trans. G. E. M. Anscombe (Oxford: Blackwell, 1953), hereafter *PI*.

[2] London: Routledge & Kegan Paul, 1922.

[3] The following, necessarily brief, general, and highly selective account of what I will be calling 'resolute' (as opposed to 'substantial') readings of the *Tractatus* is particularly indebted to two long, recent essays exemplifying that approach: James Conant's 'The Method of the *Tractatus*', in E. Reck (ed.), *From Frege to Wittgenstein* (Oxford: Oxford University Press, 2002); and James Conant and Cora Diamond, 'On Reading the *Tractatus* Resolutely', in M. Kolbel and B. Weiss (eds.), *Wittgenstein's Lasting Significance* (London: Routledge, 2004).

from mere gibberish: it is that which results from violations of logical syntax, from the combination of individually intelligible ingredients in an illegitimate way. By deliberately constructing such nonsensical propositions, the author of the *Tractatus* means to direct our attention towards metaphysical insights which cannot be expressed in genuine propositions, but which genuine propositions nevertheless show by virtue of their intelligibility—that is, by virtue of one or another aspect of their logical form, which they share with the reality that they are consequently capable of depicting either truly or falsely. This shared logical form, with all its metaphysical implications, might therefore be revealed by the necessarily hopeless attempt to speak in a manner which refuses to respect it in some specific way—by the, as it were, determinate unintelligibility of such violations of logical syntax. This gives us a way of understanding why Wittgenstein should think that speaking nonsense might nevertheless be philosophically illuminating, and hence believe that coming to recognize that certain propositions are instances of (substantial) nonsense is a criterion of philosophical insight into necessarily ineffable metaphysical truths.

An alternative way of interpreting the *Tractatus* involves what has been called an austere conception of nonsense. According to this 'resolute' reading, the author of the *Tractatus* recognized only one species of nonsense—mere gibberish; from the point of view of logic, mere nonsense is the only kind of nonsense there is. From the point of view of psychology (or culture, or history), however, one *can* distinguish between various kinds of nonsense; in particular, one can distinguish between those strings of empty signs which we are inclined to regard as substantially nonsensical from those which elicit no such inclination. In other words, certain such strings tempt us to regard them as composed from intelligible elements in unintelligible ways, and so can tempt us to think that the specific way in which they fail to make sense offers us a glimpse of (a specific aspect of) the ineffable essence of language, thought, and reality.

From the point of view of logic, however, no such species of potentially illuminating nonsense is identifiable. To determine the meaning of any sub-propositional expression, we must determine the contribution it makes to the sense of the proposition in which it figures; but if a putative proposition is in fact nonsense, it has no sense or meaning; hence, we have no way of identifying its logically significant parts—from the point of view of logic, it has none, and could have none. But the notion of substantial nonsense simultaneously requires that a 'proposition' have no meaning (otherwise it wouldn't be a species of nonsense), and yet that it be composed of individually meaningful components (otherwise it would not violate logical syntax in its way of combining those components, and so would not be distinguishable from mere gibberish).

In the terminology of the *Tractatus* (cf. 6.32–6.321) we must distinguish carefully between signs (understood as orthographic units, that which the perceptible expressions for propositions have in common) and symbols (logical units, signs in use—items belonging to a given logical category). But once we do, we see that a substantially nonsensical proposition would have to be (*qua* nonsense) a string of signs that fails to symbolize, and yet (*qua* substantial) be composed of symbols rather than mere signs—symbols whose identification presupposes that the string of signs as a whole must symbolize in a particular way, that is, say something. For a string of signs to count as a violation of logical syntax, we would have to be able to identify its components as symbolizing in logically incompatible ways. For example, Michael Dummett has offered 'Chairman Mao is rare' as a piece of substantial nonsense, because he claims it attempts to conjoin a proper name (which can take only first-level functions as arguments) with a second-level function (which can take only first-level functions as arguments).[4]

---

[4] Cf. Michael Dummett, *Frege: Philosophy of Language*, 2nd edn. (London: Duckworth, 1983), 51.

But if it is essential to a symbol's being a proper name that it take first-level functions as arguments, then we can treat 'Chairman Mao' as a proper name in this context only if we treat 'is rare' as a first-level function rather than a second-level function (say, as meaning 'tender' or 'sensitive'). And by the same token, if it is essential to a symbol's being a second-level function that it take first-level functions as arguments, then we can treat 'is rare' as a second-level function in this context only if we treat 'Chairman Mao' as a first-level function rather than a proper name (perhaps on the model of 'a brutal politician'). Either way of parsing the string of signs is perfectly feasible—we need only to determine a suitable meaning for the complementary component in each case; but each way presupposes an interpretation of the string as a whole which excludes the other. So treating it as substantial nonsense involves hovering between two feasible but incompatible ways of treating the string, without ever settling on either.

Hence, according to the resolute reading, when Wittgenstein suggests that identifying his own propositions as nonsense is a criterion for coming to understand him, he means coming to recognize that even what seems to be substantial nonsense is in fact no more than mere gibberish. He has not been about the business of identifying ineffable truths that he means to convey to us by violating the rules of logical syntax. He means, rather, to wean us away from the illusion that there are any ineffable truths—and in particular from the final, most tenacious version of that illusion, according to which, even after recognizing that genuinely ineffable truths must lie beyond the limits of language and thought, we continue to think that they might be hinted at or gestured towards, and so that we might see beyond those limits, by the deliberate construction of self-destructing pieces of nonsense. He does so by first appearing to share our conviction that there are such ineffable truths, then inviting us to discover and reflect upon the emptiness of these putative thoughts in all their versions, and then—finally—encouraging us to let go of the very idea that philosophy might be possessed of any such subject-matter. His aim is to show us that philosophy can only be an activity—the activity of identifying when and how we succumb to the temptation of thinking that we can somehow reach beyond the limits of language and thought.

In effect, then, for the resolute reading of the *Tractatus*, the substantial reading of it embodies the last and most important version of the philosophical illusion that the book aims in reality to identify and extirpate. But that means that the *Tractatus* has to traffic in the very illusion that is its target: it must deliberately construct examples of the kind of nonsense that we will be tempted to regard as substantial, if its therapeutic goal is ultimately to be attained; and that in turn means that, from Wittgenstein's point of view, this kind of nonsense is such that, properly employed, it might merit the label 'illuminating'. But it is vital to note that what makes it illuminating is not anything about the nonsense itself—nothing intrinsic to it, as it were—since logically speaking it has no intrinsic structure; it is no different in (logical) kind from any other sort of gibberish. It does, however, exemplify a distinctive psychological kind of nonsense, one that has a certain kind of appeal to us; and hence it can play a philosophically illuminating role in a specific kind of therapeutic interchange between author and reader.

Accordingly, one distinguishing characteristic of a resolute reading of the *Tractatus* is that it does not take those propositions of the *Tractatus* that Wittgenstein refers to in 6.54 as 'nonsensical' to convey ineffable insights. The second key distinguishing characteristic is a rejection of the idea that recognizing the nonsensicality of these or any other propositions requires the application of a theory of meaning—a specification of the conditions under which a sentence makes sense—that is advanced in the body of the work. According to resolute readers, there is no such theory to be found in the book, and according to the book's own lights, there could be no such theory. For to what would such a theory be applied? Suppose we imagine someone claiming that the author of the *Tractatus* advances bipolarity as a condition for the sense or meaningfulness of a proposition (let's leave tautologies and contradictions aside for the moment), and so licenses us to dismiss any non-bipolar proposition as nonsense; and now recall the key *Tractatus* distinction between signs and symbols. The question arises: what is it that lacks bipolarity—a string of signs or a complex of symbols? No mere string of signs could possibly either possess or lack bipolarity; but if we are in a position to treat some given string of signs as symbolizing, then we must have parsed it as symbolizing in a particular way, and hence assigned specific logical roles to its components. If so, then the question of whether or not it possesses bipolarity comes too late; and if not—if, that is, we haven't yet settled on a particular parsing of it—then that question simply doesn't arise.

In other words, before any general doctrine about non-bipolar propositions can be brought to bear on a particular candidate, before we are even in a position to think of ourselves as having a candidate that might meet this proposed criterion for nonsensicality, we must already have made clear the particular use we are inclined to make of it such that we want to say of it that it expresses something non-bipolar (and that it is not a tautology, and so on). In other words, all the work is being done by that process of clarification of meaning, not by the attempted application of a general doctrine to whatever is thereby clarified; and if the proposition-like thing is philosophically problematic, then (as with the case of 'Chairman Mao is rare') that will come out in the attempted process of clarification as a kind of failure to mean anything in particular by it, or a hovering between various ways of meaning something by it, rather than by its violating logical syntax.

In other words, a resolute reading of the *Tractatus* sees it not as intended to construct a specific philosophical account of the conditions of sense, whether that account is regarded as replacing, supplementing, or merely providing a grounding for our everyday capacities for linguistic expression and understanding; it is, rather, intended simply to deploy that everyday understanding in a philosophical context. It mobilizes a certain kind of practical knowledge, a know-how possessed by anyone capable of speech, in the service of identifying and overcoming certain philosophical illusions—in particular, the illusion that our everyday understanding of language, and hence of the distinction between sense and nonsense, is in need of the support or authority of a philosophical theory.

Might one characterize this understanding as itself ineffable, and hence characterize resolute readings as attempting simultaneously to have their cake and eat it (by criticizing substantial readings for deploying an empty notion of ineffable truth, and then helping themselves to a very similar conception)[5]? In one sense, no: for according to the resolute reading, the ability to recognize the distinction between sense and nonsense—what one might call our capacity to acknowledge the limits of intelligibility—is not a matter of grasping ineffable necessary truths about language, thought, and reality. It is simply the capacity to recognize when a sign has not been given a determinate meaning—even when it appears that it has been. In another sense, however, the practical know-how we are thereby drawing upon is such that any attempt to state it in words will produce an utterance that anyone who possesses that know-how must recognize as itself nonsensical. In this sense, the understanding is ineffable: but that is not because its object or content is a species of ineffable truth; and its ineffability in would-be declarative utterances does not amount to its ineffability *per se*—since its presence is directly manifest in a certain kind of practical ability, including the ability to distinguish nonsense from sense in the domain of philosophical discourse.

Huge controversy has surrounded the advocacy of resolute readings of the *Tractatus*: some think it is internally incoherent, others that it misrepresents important aspects of the text, and

---

[5] This is a possibility raised in a recent, extremely illuminating and helpful exchange between Adrian Moore and Peter Sullivan, entitled 'Ineffability and Nonsense', in *Proceedings of the Aristotelian Society*, supp. vol. 77, (2003), 169–223.

still others that it is rebutted by a range of Wittgenstein's later comments on his early work (indeed, some critics endorse all three kinds of objection). Much debate has focused on the question of whether resolute readers are right to think that much mainstream commentary on the *Tractatus* ever since its publication has in fact amounted to a set of variations upon a substantial reading of it. I cannot address these criticisms at the appropriate level of detail here; but I hope that I have done enough to show that it is at least arguable that resolute readings are both coherent and well-grounded in the text. In the present context, what interests me most is that proponents of the resolute reading have identified a *possible* misreading of the *Tractatus*—an inherently tempting way of missing its fundamental point whilst remaining deeply convinced that one has grasped it.

In the light cast by resolute readings, one might characterize this fundamental point as that of identifying and aiming to overcome our attraction to the idea that there is something we cannot do in philosophy. The notion of substantial nonsense is that of pseudo-propositions that are unintelligible, but determinately so; they therefore seem to specify a thought that we cannot think—an identifiable place in the region that lies beyond the limits of sense, something specific that exceeds our mental grasp. But of course, if the limits of sense are the limits of intelligibility, then nothing whatever lies beyond them; they are not boundaries fencing us off from a further determinate or determinable region, and so not limitations upon our capacity to think or speak. To recognize that the only species of nonsense is gibberish is, accordingly, to recognize that the limits of sense are not limitations; to acknowledge them as limits rather than limitations is precisely a matter of acknowledging that there is nothing (no specifiable thing, no conceivable task or activity) that we cannot do.

If we cast the fundamental point of the *Tractatus* in these terms, of course, we can see at least the possibility of one particular kind of continuity between the intended task of Wittgenstein's early philosophy and that of his later work, as that finds expression in the *Philosophical Investigations*. Take, for example, the following remarks:

The great difficulty here is not to represent the matter as if there were something one *couldn't* do. (*PI* §374)

When a sentence is called senseless, it is not as it were its sense that is senseless. But a combination of words is being excluded from the language, withdrawn from circulation. (*PI* §500)

If we regard the notion of 'grammar' invoked in the later work as Wittgenstein's way of recalling us to the distinction between sense and nonsense, and we disregard the words of warning I have just cited, then invoking grammar in order to identify and reject certain philosophical utterances as nonsense might be thought to involve treating such nonsense as substantial—that is, as determinately unintelligible, as if its nonsensicality is a result of the speaker attempting to conjoin intelligible words in unintelligible ways (conjunctions which violate their grammar, as opposed to violating their logical syntax). After all, one might think, how can we know that the philosopher cannot say or think what he wants to say or think, without knowing what exactly it is that he wants to say or think? But if so, then we are on the verge of presenting grammar as prohibiting the philosopher from saying or thinking something in particular. Such ways of understanding Wittgenstein's later philosophy would thereby suggest that it involves recognizing that there are things that we cannot do—that grammatical reminders articulate the limits of sense, and thereby identify a region or domain that lies beyond those limits, from which we are excluded. It may further lead us to assume that his later grammatical investigations presuppose or otherwise deploy an implicit philosophical theory of the (now grammatical) conditions of sense—quite as if our everyday abilities to distinguish sense from nonsense require at the very least a philosophical grounding or foundation (perhaps a criterial semantics, or a theory of language-games, or an anthropology of the human form of life).

A properly resolute reading of the *Philosophical Investigations* would regard the above kind of reading of the book as attributing to it a conception of nonsense which is in fact one of its central targets. Such a reading will therefore attempt to understand grammatical investigation as simply deploying our everyday capacity to distinguish sense from nonsense in a philosophical context, and hence as depriving itself of any claim to expertise or authority that exceeds that form of practical ability—an ability that can equally well be laid claim to by any competent speaker, and hence by any philosophical interlocutor. It will, in short, see the primary task of the later philosophy as a matter of identifying and attempting to overcome our sense that grammar is a limitation on our capacities for speech and thought—that it deprives us of something. It will, in effect, amount to the same project of acknowledging (as opposed to despairing of, resenting, or denying) our finitude that resolute readers find always already at work in the *Tractatus*.

Once again, I am not much interested in claiming that any particular mainstream readings of the *Philosophical Investigations* would count as substantial rather than resolute in the sense just specified—although I take it to be obvious that some would. What matters is that the very nature of the philosophical terrain here makes a substantial reading of grammar, and hence of the nature and authority of grammatical investigations, a real possibility, and one that poses a particularly significant obstacle to the business of gaining a proper hearing for Wittgenstein's later conception of philosophy. For those who succumb to it will seem to say precisely what Wittgenstein says; they will be able to cite Wittgenstein in their own defence, to deploy his distinctive terminology and remind us of his distinctive terms of criticism, since they have at least correctly identified the distinctive domain of his concerns—the business of distinguishing sense from nonsense, the field of grammatical investigation. But they will mean what they say, and what they cite Wittgenstein as saying, otherwise: from the perspective of the resolute reading, they will in fact betray the enterprise from within, by attempting to further it in a way that constitutes its inner destruction. For their way of urging us not to treat grammatical limits as limitations will ineluctably convey to us the sense that there is something we cannot do.

One resolute reader has explicitly argued that Wittgenstein's remarks on the idea of a private language might be seen as an illuminating test-case for the claim that even those genuinely sympathetic to his later work can find themselves defending it in terms, and with a tenor, that amounts to its subversion into substantiality.[6] In my view, the specific details of James Conant's avowedly brief and highly general attempt to characterize that case in such terms seriously hinder his chances of convincing a general audience of its accuracy. For he makes it integral to his specification of a substantial reading of these remarks that it regard grammatical remarks or reminders as putative truths (whether genuinely necessary truths, or ultimately contingent ones, is then held to be a point of essential instability in the self-understanding of the substantial reader). Since, however, the mainstream commentator he specifies as paradigmatically substantial—Peter Hacker—has consistently argued that grammatical 'propositions' must be understood as a species of rule or norm, in relation to which the concept of truth is explicitly held to have no place, his argument is bound to appear to miss its central target.[7]

Nevertheless, I share Conant's general conviction that the ways in which one reads this particular stretch of the *Investigations* can provide a particularly clear and helpful illustration of the strength of the temptation to misread the philosophical method manifest in the book as a whole in this manner, and of the importance of diagnosing and overcoming that temptation. Accordingly, the

[6] James Conant, 'Why Worry about the *Tractatus?*', in B. Stocker (ed.), *Post-Analytic Tractatus* (Aldershot: Ashgate, 2004), esp. 171–7.

[7] Conant's specific focus is Hacker's massively influential *Analytical Commentary on the* Philosophical Investigations (Oxford: Blackwell, 1980, 1986, 1990, and 1996), the first two volumes of which he wrote with Gordon Baker.

primary preoccupation of this essay is that of critically evaluating the philosophical illumination that might be gained by attempting to transfer this originally Tractarian distinction between resolute and substantial readings to the context of Wittgenstein's later philosophy. In making any such attempt, however, it soon becomes clear that reference to Stanley Cavell's work on the *Philosophical Investigations* is indispensable; for, as resolute readers of the *Tractatus* have always acknowledged, some (although interestingly, not all) of his readings of key passages on the idea of a private language are precisely attuned to the danger of representing the situation as one in which there is something that we cannot do. Accordingly, the second of my orienting concerns in this essay is a critical evaluation of Stanley Cavell's highly distinctive interpretation of this stretch of Wittgenstein's text.

Whilst Cavell is now increasingly well known as an interpreter of Wittgenstein, it is (I believe) far less well known that he has developed over the years a sustained, highly original and extremely significant reading of the most famous of Wittgenstein's remarks on privacy and language. There are several reasons for this lack of recognition, beyond the still-prevalent misunderstandings of his general philosophical stance that I attempted to rebut in an earlier work.[8] One is that Cavell himself has expressed a certain disquiet at the canonical status attributed to §243–315 with respect to Wittgenstein's treatment of these particular themes: 'I find little said within these inventions, especially about privacy and about language, that is not said, generally more clearly, elsewhere in the *Investigations*, so that the very fame of this argument suggests to me that it has been miscast'[9]. Another is that Cavell's various remarks about the remarks in this stretch of text are scattered throughout his writings—from early articles, through *The Claim of Reason*, to

---

[8] See my *Stanley Cavell: Philosophy's Recounting of the Ordinary* (Oxford: Oxford University Press, 1994).

[9] Stanley Cavell, *The Claim of Reason* (Oxford: Oxford University Press, 1979), 342; hereafter *CR*.

more recent essays and lectures—and this has conspired against the possibility of taking them in as a perspicuous whole.

In this essay, accordingly, I will attempt to bring the most important of these responses together, within a relatively small compass, in order to revive this possibility, to demonstrate the extent to which each intervention takes support from as well as supporting the others, and thereby to make possible a proper critical evaluation of each remark, and so of the strengths and weaknesses of the overall interpretative approach that generates them. It is a real question for me whether doing so runs contrary to the spirit of Cavell's own mode of engagement with this part of Wittgenstein's work, and in particular whether it may involve an unwise discounting of Cavell's disquiet about the fame of this sequence of sections. What allays this anxiety to some extent are the following observations. First, if the prevailing ways of interpreting these remarks do indeed miscast them, then that is worth knowing; but it cannot be established except by engaging in detail with them. And second, what results from that detailed engagement in the light of Cavell's own remarks is the conviction that things are said, and insights attained, here that are not in fact said or attained in exactly these ways elsewhere in the *Investigations*. And since what is said is not, in Cavell's eyes as in my own, sharply distinguishable from how it is said, that amounts to a reason for continuing to regard these remarks as an indispensable part of Wittgenstein's philosophical project.

This point about the relation between form and content in philosophical writing prompts me to note that this essay has a third underlying aim or concern. For its precise textual focus is such that it amounts to a continuation of the reading of Wittgenstein's *Philosophical Investigations* that I began in Part I of my *Inheritance and Originality*.[10] That initial reading began with the opening of the *Investigations*, and continued unbroken to §242, where—instead

---

[10] Oxford: Oxford University Press, 2001.

of following the text's shift from rule-following to the idea of a private language—I shifted instead to the much later discussion of seeing aspects, which occupies the largest section of Part II of the *Investigations*. My main reason for doing so was that it allowed me to show that, and how, certain concepts that crop up insistently in Wittgenstein's remarks about seeing-as could be seen as recountings of—that is, as at once reiterating and reconceiving the results of—his earlier remarks about following rules, with all their relevance to the question of what is involved in knowing how to go on with words. I never, however, saw any reason to think that the more intuitively obvious way of going on with my own reading—that of going on with Wittgenstein's words in the order in which he arranged them for us—was in any way unfeasible, or unlikely to produce further illumination. Indeed, one reason for now returning to follow that more natural path is precisely to demonstrate that the same themes that emerged from my reading of the first 242 sections of the *Investigations* can be seen to maintain their prominence in, and governance of, the subsequent stretch of text—§243–315—so often taken to be canonical in Wittgenstein's investigation of the idea, or fantasy, of a private language. In particular, I want to show that these sections reveal a similarly internal relation between the form and the content of Wittgenstein's investigations—a relation that is required by his distinctively perfectionist, and hence therapeutic, relation with his readers. This places an unusually high premium on the exploitation of what one might call the more literary dimensions of language (especially the resources of figuration, imagery, and metaphor, often deployed in the telling of imaginative tales); more particularly, it involves Wittgenstein in repeated returns to a certain range of such resources (for example, the recurrent emergence of images of machinery or the mechanical in our philosophical pictures of language, our relations with language, and our nature as human beings).

There are, of course, manifest links between this matter and my interest in Cavell. To begin with, the general tenor of my approach to the *Investigations* in *Inheritance and Originality* reflected lessons I have learnt from Cavell's work in the past, about Wittgenstein in particular and about philosophy in general. Cavell's recovery of a non-elitist model of perfectionism, in ethics and in philosophy, was perhaps the most important of these lessons; and it continues in the present reading. But more specifically, in pursuing the ways in which Cavell's writing, as well as that of Wittgenstein, both aligns itself with and distances itself from the Tractarian paradigm of austere nonsense, I found that those (failures of) alignment importantly involve an attunement to the figurative dimensions of grammatical investigations—in short, to the philosophical relevance of exercises of the imagination in relation to our ways with words. In short, this essay has been shaped by the conviction that no one of my three orienting concerns can be pursued without pursuing the other two.

I

Wittgenstein's Monologuists (§243)

A human being can encourage himself, give himself orders, obey, blame and punish himself; he can ask himself a question and answer it. We could even imagine human beings who spoke only in monologue; who accompanied their activities by talking to themselves.—An explorer who watched them and listened to their talk might succeed in translating their language into ours. (This would enable him to predict these people's actions correctly, for he also hears them making resolutions and decisions.)

But could we also imagine a language in which a person could write down or give vocal expression to his inner experiences—his feelings, moods, and the rest—for his private use?— —Well, can't we do so in our ordinary language?—But that is not what I mean. The individual words of this language are to refer to what can only be known to the person speaking; to his immediate private sensations. So another person cannot understand the language. (*PI* §243)

Having overheard the provisional resolution of these exchanges within Wittgenstein's consciousness, can we think of ourselves as having successfully grasped what he means by a 'private language'? If so, would we not be able to foresee the textual actions that will ensue—predict the specific twists and turns of the further questions and answers, directions and self-criticisms, that follow from this new beginning of his philosophical investigations? However, it will soon appear that each such turn can be interpreted so as to be consistent with two different readings of that opening exchange. Hence, if we get off on one foot as readers, our further explorations will not demand that we return to the beginning and try the other; but Wittgenstein's writing will always hold open the possibility of another way of going on with it, and hence always resist our desire to view our own way as necessary, or fated.

Here is one way of reading the second paragraph of § 243. The first sentence sketches an idea—that of using language to give voice to our inner experiences for our personal use—and the rest of the paragraph distinguishes two different ways of filling it out. The first is exemplified by our ordinary life with language, when keeping a journal, writing a memoir, composing a love poem, and so on; but Wittgenstein swiftly rejects this as not what he means. The final two sentences specify what he does mean: the idea of a language whose words refer to the speaker's immediate, private sensations, and hence whose meaning can be known only to that speaker. This idea, and the philosophical issues it puts in play, are the topic of the succeeding sections of the text.

Here is another way of reading that second paragraph. The first sentence asks whether we can imagine—literally, find thinkable the idea of—a language in which someone can express his inner experiences for his personal use. There is then a double-dash in the text—an unusually long pause, as if Wittgenstein needs time to contemplate what has just been said. Then he responds by reminding his interlocutor (reminding himself) that we do just this in ordinary language. Giving voice to our inner life for our own purposes is a commonplace of our life with words. How, then, can any participant in that life find himself asking whether we can imagine such a thing, thereby implying that its very intelligibility is questionable, when it is a humdrum actuality? His interlocutor then hastily replies that this everyday banality is not at all what he meant; and in the final two sentences of the paragraph, he attempts to explain what he really wanted the words of the first sentence to mean. And in the following sections, Wittgenstein tries to determine whether this attempt is really successful—whether there is a way of meaning the words of the penultimate sentence that does not simply return us to a banality, whether in fact his interlocutor means anything in particular by those words.

If we follow through with the first (call it the substantial) reading of § 243, then the most famous succeeding sections—§§244, 246, 253, and 258—constitute points at which Wittgenstein shows that, given the meaning of the words in the interlocutor's penultimate sentence, the idea of a private language that he attempts to construct out of them must be nonsensical or incoherent, a violation of grammar. § 244 unfolds the grammar of 'referring' to 'sensations'; §§ 246 and 253 remind us of the grammar of the 'privacy' of 'sensations'; and § 258 recalls the grammatical conditions for meaning, and hence for the applicability of the terms 'words' and 'language', thereby showing that the private linguist cannot legitimately appropriate them. In effect, then, recollecting the meaning of the words 'referring', 'private', 'sensation', 'word', and 'language' shows us that the interlocutor's talk of 'a language whose words are to refer to the private sensations of the speaker' is no more than a nonsensical combination of words. And we are then invited to ask why we might have felt driven to violate grammar in this particular way.

If we follow through with the second (call it the resolute) reading of §243, then those succeeding sections appear as points at which Wittgenstein tries to imagine, and then tries out, ways of giving meaning to the constituent terms of the interlocutor's formulation. Since the conclusion of §243 gives us only a form of words, together with a strenuous rejection of one way of understanding it, the succeeding investigations must determine whether there is any other way of taking them that might give them genuine substance. In so far as Wittgenstein's attempts to imagine such ways fail to satisfy his interlocutor—in so far as the interlocutor's implicit response to these attempts reiterates his response to Wittgenstein's first such attempt in §243, viz 'But that is not what I mean'—then what the interlocutor does mean remains undetermined. He is left with a form of words, and a variety of ways in which they might coherently be taken; but none of those ways satisfy him—none capture what he had it at heart to say. It remains open to him to imagine another such way, and thereby to find the satisfaction he seeks; but if he does not, then Wittgenstein implicitly invites him to ask himself why he is passionately convinced that his words mean something in particular—indeed something deeply significant about our inner life and our expressions of it—and yet rejects any particular assignment of meaning to his words.

In support of the resolute reading, we might stress that Wittgenstein repeatedly begins his investigation of the interlocutor's formulations by asking what their elements might mean, rather than telling us what they do mean. §244 begins with him asking 'How do words *refer* to sensations?', and ends by canvassing what he calls 'one possible way' to give content to that italicized term; §246 begins by asking 'In what sense are my sensations private?', and continues in response to one answer that Wittgenstein imagines his interlocutor might give; §253 begins with another imagined remark by the interlocutor (' "Another person can't have my pains" '), and continues by asking what the constituent terms of this remark might mean ('Which are *my* pains?'), and considering possible answers. If, however, we wanted to support the substantial reading, we might emphasize the numerous occasions on which Wittgenstein seems not so much to exercise his imagination on his interlocutor's behalf, but rather to lay down the law to him. In §244, we are simply told that 'the verbal expression of pain replaces crying and does not describe it'; in §246, we learn that 'The truth is: it makes sense to say about other people that they doubt whether I am in pain; but not to say it about myself'; and in §253, that 'one does not define a criterion of identity by emphatic stressing of the word "this" '.

Moreover, each way of reading Wittgenstein will have its own ways of accommodating those aspects of his text that appear to speak in favour of the opposed way of reading it. Substantial readers can always interpret Wittgenstein's reliance on questions and suggestions and assertions voiced by his interlocutor as merely rhetorical devices preparing the ground for the full-throated declarations that constitute Wittgenstein's own desire to reclaim his interlocutor for the common ground of ordinary meanings. Likewise, resolute readers can always interpret Wittgenstein's apparently decisive grammatical reminders as essentially responsive to possibilities invoked by his interlocutor, and hence as invitations to acknowledge that his imagined projections of his words either have implications that will not satisfy him, or are in fact insufficiently substantial or contentful to generate definite implications.

Since each reading can therefore point to an aspect of the text that it fully acknowledges, and whose proper acknowledgement by the other is at the very least an issue for it, it would seem profitless to insist that one reading is essentially faithful to Wittgenstein's text and the other intrinsically faithless. Perhaps its author rather means to make possible both ways of reading it—to give us two apparently different ways of reaching the conclusion that the private linguist has failed to invoke anything in particular in attempting to invoke the 'idea' of a private language, and to force us to ask whether it matters which way we dramatize the process of reaching that conclusion. Since both readings acknowledge that the interlocutor resists the ordinary meanings of his words, and both claim that he fails to specify any coherent and satisfying alternative way of taking them, what difference does it make whether we present these acknowledgements and claims as earned by recalling us to our ordinary life with words, or by recounting ways in which we might imagine that we can repudiate it? Is it perhaps essential to Wittgenstein's conception of philosophical prose as unassertive that it avoid declaring this fact about itself—that it not insist on its uninsistence? If so, it cannot simply assert that an assertive reading of itself is wrong. Or perhaps that conception cannot eliminate an assertive moment in its imaginative engagements with emptiness, any more than grammatical reminders can eschew normativity. If so, what we really need is a reading that does not assume or present those aspects of the text upon which substantial and resolute readers respectively fasten as occluding each other, or as ones between which we must choose.

However we answer this question, it is one concerning the relation between form and content in Wittgenstein's writing; hence it forces us to investigate not only his treatment of the idea of a private language, but also his idea of how one should treat any philosophical problem, and the one in relation to the other—each as if called for by the other. It is, accordingly, worth highlighting something implicit in my opening response to Wittgenstein's way of opening his investigation of this idea. For whilst it is not wrong to read the first paragraph of §243 as describing an explorer's encounter with an imaginary tribe of monologuists, it would not be right entirely to overlook the fact that Wittgenstein's imagination takes off from a reminder about the ways in which our ordinary life with language can take a multitude of reflexive forms. And the particular reflexive forms he mentions (encouraging, ordering and obeying, blaming, punishing, questioning and answering oneself) amount to a portrait in miniature of the characteristic stylistic forms of the *Philosophical Investigations*—on the entirely plausible assumption that Wittgenstein's interlocutory dialogues are also internal or self-addressed, an enactment of his conception of philosophizing as exemplary self-examination, as a matter of taking oneself as other to oneself, as subject to inclinations and compulsions that one can also subject to question and criticism, and that, however personal, always seem able to elicit the recognition of others.

On such a reading, when Wittgenstein's imaginative anthropological extrapolation of our ordinary capacity to talk to ourselves conjures up an explorer (*einem Forscher*) who encounters exclusively monolingual speakers, that explorer might equally well be thought of—his purpose might equally well be translated as that of—a researcher or searcher, even an inquirer or investigator into a distinctive mode or circle of philosophizing, and hence into its participants' ways of going on; he might more precisely be thought of as Wittgenstein's portrait of his reader.

This in turn suggests that Wittgenstein thinks that the reflexive nature of his own writing—its utter dependence upon our everyday capacity to examine our ways of giving voice to ourselves—naturally engenders a fantasy or a fear of giving voice to oneself in a way that goes beyond the resources of the everyday, beyond anyone else's capacity to comprehend. Perhaps the language that Wittgenstein is trying to forge for his philosophical purposes, as the diary-like entries of his notebooks are transfigured into the numbered sections of the *Investigations,* depends upon a conception of the self (as knowable and expressible and communicable by at least an imaginative reshaping of our ordinary linguistic resources) that is itself subject to philosophical critique? And if language can be private in a sense other than that familiar from our journals and love poetry, is Wittgenstein's philosophical discourse fated to miss its goals? Can his interior monologues for more than one voice ever truly speak to or for another, and hence elicit a genuine philosophical dialogue? Can we explorers of his texts ever really succeed in translating his language into ours?

2

A Child is Crying (§§244–5)

Wittgenstein begins his response to the very idea of a private language by imagining a question that might be prompted by its initial articulation.

How do words *refer* to sensations?—There doesn't seem to be any problem here; don't we talk about sensations every day, and give them names? But how is the connexion between the name and the thing named set up? This question is the same as: how does a human being learn the meaning of the names of sensations?—of the word "pain" for example. Here is one possibility: words are connected with the primitive, the natural, expressions of the sensation and used in their place. A child has hurt himself and he cries; and then adults talk to him and teach him exclamations and, later, sentences. They teach the child new pain-behaviour.

"So you are saying that the word 'pain' really means crying?"—On the contrary: the verbal expression of pain replaces crying and does not describe it.

For how can I go so far as to try to use language to get between pain and its expression? (*PI* §§244–5)

In §243, the idea of a private language is characterized as one whose individual words refer to the speaker's immediate private sensations; so §244 begins by forcing us explicitly to contemplate this apparently self-evident notion of 'reference'. More specifically, it speaks on behalf of someone suddenly struck by a sense of difficulty or puzzlement with the very idea of reference in this context.

Wittgenstein immediately emphasizes (in apparently resolute vein) that naming and otherwise talking about our sensations is an everyday phenomenon—as much a commonplace of our life with words as is giving expression to our feelings or moods for our private use. If we look at that aspect of ordinary life, we will see—it will be manifest—how words refer to sensations, how sensation-words fit into (that is, how they resemble and differ from, and how they are interwoven with) our life with other kinds of words, and hence with language and with reality. How, then, might we come to be gripped by a sense that the very intelligibility of this humdrum actuality is questionable? The interlocutor attempts to clarify his sense of difficulty: it concerns how, in this context, we can set up the connection between name and thing named at all—how the connections manifest in our everyday talk about sensations might be effected in the first place.

Wittgenstein's second response to his interlocutor offers (more accurately, it imposes) a reinterpretation of his reformulated question: he flatly asserts that it is equivalent to asking how human beings learn the meaning of sensation-words. Is this interpretative imposition justified? Is the interlocutor's initial sense of bewilderment about the sheer existence of a naming or reference relation between words and sensations really being given adequate expression when reformulated as an apparently empirical question about how someone might learn the meaning of such words; or does this forced equation rather conceal the initial difficulty? After all, if his bewilderment is not eased by a reminder of the self-evident fact that people do talk about sensations, why should it be eased by a reminder of the equally self-evident fact that people do learn how to engage in such talk (let alone by any more specific claims about how they learn to do so)? His question is: how is any of this so much as possible?

But if the interlocutor's difficulty really is well captured by his own reformulation of it, which articulates the issue as one of how the relevant connection is 'set up' (say, established or effected, brought about), then the most natural (a substantial reader might say, the only established) way of taking his question is as one about how that connection is made by or for any given speaker—that is, as a question about language acquisition, about teaching and learning. And if (as a resolute reader might be willing to consider) it is not to be so taken, then the interlocutor owes us an account of how it can and should be taken otherwise. On this latter reading, then, Wittgenstein's response to that reformulation is designed to reveal that, unless the notion of 'setting up' is given a concrete context of application, it remains entirely lacking in content. By so flatly denying any other way of taking the notion, Wittgenstein resists, and so invites us to reconsider, our sense that there really is an issue (one that the interlocutor is striving to articulate) concerning the sheer possibility of the connectedness of sensation-words and sensations as such—an issue that is somehow more fundamental than, essentially prior to, and so not to be identified with, any concrete question about how those specific kinds of word–world connection are in fact established. In short, Wittgenstein is, from the outset, concerned to emphasize the naturalness, and the uncannily rapid unfolding, of our desire to sublime the notions of reference and naming—our compulsion to mean them, but in no particular way.

This process of sublimation is further contested by Wittgenstein's apparently casual introduction of 'pain' as the particular sensation-word with respect to which a possible answer to the interlocutor's reinterpreted question will be sought. For it is part of his purpose to imply that, just as the interlocutor is tempted to invoke the notion of 'setting up connections' between sensation-words and sensations without committing himself to any particular way of employing it, so his invocation of the notion of 'sensation-words' (and hence of sensations) threatens to floats free of concrete reality in so far as he refrains from specifying which particular sensation-word is under discussion. For there may be no single, uniform, or homogeneous story to be told about how all sensation-words are learnt; different sensation-words might be acquired in different (although related or overlapping) ways. Accordingly, to focus on one particular example further forces the interlocutor to confront the realities to which his account must ultimately be responsive.

By the same token, however, in so far as the choice of 'pain' is his, rather than his interlocutor's, Wittgenstein must take responsibility for the concreteness of the particular example upon which so much of the rest of his famous discussion famously focuses. He must, in particular, take care to distinguish between conclusions that hold about that particular example, and conclusions that might generalize beyond it, and between the varying extents to which any given conclusion does in fact generalize—immediately within the realm of sensations, but more broadly across the terrain of psychological phenomena (for example, to the feelings and moods mentioned in §243). It is not possible to determine in advance how, and how far, one's choice of example might inflect one's investigation here; but that it will do so, and with potentially fateful consequences, is surely beyond contestation.

On the face of it, of course, 'pain' seems an eminently suitable example for present purposes—by which I mean both Wittgenstein's purposes and those of his interlocutor(s). It is, to begin with, surely the most insistently self-evident of sensations, and one with strong links to human physiology on the one hand and to expressive behaviour on the other. The pertinence of these features will become clear as we go along, but it is noteworthy that proponents of otherwise radically different positions in the philosophy of mind have tended (perhaps rather too readily) to agree on the suitability of pain as an example of the phenomena in which they all have an interest. Without denying any of this, however, we might wonder whether Wittgenstein's choice of this example is more specifically motivated.

For example, 'pain' is etymologically linked (via the Latin root *poena*, penalty or punishment) to the various reflexive uses of language that initially motivate the anxiety about private language in §243—certainly to those of blaming and punishing; plausibly to those of issuing and obeying orders, and encouraging oneself (understood as seeking courage in the face of threatened suffering, perhaps by threatening to inflict suffering on oneself); possibly to that of interrogating oneself (understood as putting oneself on trial, even perhaps as part of a form of self-torture). Would this justify us in seeing a connection between Wittgenstein's investigations into the ways in which we do, and can, found meaning on sensations of pain, and Nietzsche's investigations into the meanings we have given our pain—in particular, what he sees as our Christian interpretation of human pain as punishment (not just for wrongdoing but for the sheer fact of our existence), and his interpretation of us as preferring the self-punishment of such interpretations to suffering the realization that pain has no meaning, that it neither embodies nor founds any structure of significance? Perhaps we should rather restrict ourselves to considering the possibility that Wittgenstein sees connections between the construction of a fantasy of private expression and the suffering and infliction of pain—whether because the experience of suffering pain engenders a vision of insuperable isolation, or because such fantasies amount to a form of self-punishment (for example, a denial of access to others), or because constructing a philosophical inquiry in which to give expression to such self-understandings demands that he risk obedience to a form of self-interrogation that threatens to exact penalties of extreme psychological and disciplinary isolation. But perhaps the last of these possibilities brings us once again into rather too close a proximity to Nietzsche.

Suppose, then, we return to Witttgenstein's proposed answer to the question of how human beings learn the meaning of 'pain'. The heart of it lies in what amounts to a reorientation or displacement of the notion of a connection invoked by his interlocutor. For the connection Wittgenstein emphasizes is not between sensation-words and sensations, but between wordless cries, exclamations, and sentences involving sensation-words; and the kind of connection in play is not that of attaching a linguistic label to a non-linguistic thing, but that of linguistic expressions replacing or displacing—anyway, being used in the place of—natural, non-linguistic, behavioural expressions or manifestations of sensations. In short, the key connection is not between inner and outer, but within the realm of the outer, between public phenomena. But Wittgenstein's point is not that sensation-words do not really refer to sensations; it is rather that to say that sensation-words are names just *is* to say that they function as learnt replacements for unlearnt expressive behaviour. One might say: in this dimension of our life with language, naming or reference is a function of expression.

More specifically, the connection between 'pain' and pain is set up in a manner which exploits the natural human repertoire of expressive behaviour, the fact that pain naturally finds expression in certain forms of behaviour—so that, for example, when 'A child has hurt himself, he cries'. The language of pain is grafted on to a more primitive exclamatory language, which is itself grafted on to wordless manifestations of pain; the establishment of a referential relation between 'pain' and pain therefore depends upon the naturally established relation between pain and its expression. And this precisely undercuts the assumption engendering the interlocutor's reformulated question, which presupposes that the everyday role of verbal and written expressions of pain must itself be accounted for in terms of the establishment of a naming relation between 'pain' and pain. Little wonder, then, that Wittgenstein invites us to speculate (in §245) about how we come to feel compelled to invoke such linguistic connections in order to mediate, or otherwise ground, a connection (between pain and the forms of behaviour expressive of it) that requires no such intermediary—in short, to try to do something that cannot be done because there is no gap to bridge, no connection to forge, in the first place. It is quite as if we want to repress or deny the natural expressiveness of our behaviour altogether.

The idea of a graft here is also meant to indicate a combination of dependence and independence, a hybrid of the old and the new. On the one hand, to make a graft presupposes the existence of something on to which a graft can be made (no wordless cries, no language of pain); on the other hand, what results from a graft is not identical with what existed prior to its being made (sentences are not exclamations, which in turn are not cries or shrieks). This is why Wittgenstein never says that the language of pain is a species of expressive pain behaviour, for it is never simply or merely or just that; in this context, naming is a *function* of expression, not a synonym for it. In other words, even though it would not be the language of pain if it did not take the place of expressive pain behaviour, in taking on or taking over that place in our lives it transforms it by introducing indefinitely ramifying ranges of new possibilities into it—new ways of articulating one's inner experiences, ways which introduce the evaluative dimension of truth and falsehood (and so a role in the space of reasons) without expelling the expressive dimension.[1] And of course, on to each such graft further new ways can be grafted in their turn.

It is also important to see that what Wittgenstein presents here as the key connection (between natural and verbal expressions of sensations) is not itself seen and acted upon by the person whose expressions these are, but rather by those around him. The child, who hurts himself, cries; it is not he, but the adults around him, who make the connection between his cries and the domain of exclamations and sentences in the language of pain. There is no moment of recognition on his part that mediates between his pain and his crying, certainly none that involves an act of identifying or naming what he is feeling as pain (another way of trying to use language to mediate a non-existent gap between pain and its

[1] This confluence or simultaneity of expression and self-ascription in first-person psychological utterances is the central concern of David Finkelstein's excellent *Expression and the Inner* (Cambridge, Mass.: Harvard University Press; 2003).

expression). It is the adults who recognize his cries as cries of pain, and hence are in a position to replace them with primitive linguistic forms of pain behaviour, and so induct him into (this dimension of) life with language.

In other words, the relevant linguistic connection between 'pain' and pain is set up for the individual learner by the society of which he is a part. His mastery of that connection (and so his capacity to articulate his feeling even in the most primitive linguistic forms) is an effect or function of his presence in a human social world in which that connection is always already effected, or in effect. For the child can come to employ the word 'pain' with respect to himself and to others only in so far as others have already employed that term with respect to him; his first-person (as well as any subsequent third-person) uses of the term are grounded in his natural capacity to satisfy the criteria for third-person uses of the term by others. But it is not just that those others must be *able* to see his behaviour as expressive of pain; they must also be willing to do so. One might say: his cries must be seen as, acknowledged as, cries of pain by those who make up his social world if he is to receive the gift or graft of the language of pain. And if this holds of pain behaviour, it must also hold of the full range of his natural expressive repertoire, and so of his human status, in so far as that status involves the possession of an inner life that one is capable of articulating for oneself.

This idea of children acquiring language, understood as in the gift of one's elders (the German term translated as 'adults' in §244 is the same as that used to translate Augustine's *majores homines* into German—*Erwachsenen*), inevitably brings to mind the quotation with which the *Philosophical Investigations* opens:

When they (my elders) named some object, and accordingly moved towards something, I saw this and I grasped that the thing was called by the sound they uttered when they meant to point it out. Their intention was shewn by their bodily movements, as it were the natural language of all peoples: the expression of the face, the play of the eyes, the movement of other parts of the body, and the tone of voice which expresses our state of mind in seeking, having, rejecting, or avoiding something. Thus, as I heard words repeatedly used in their proper places in various sentences, I gradually learnt to understand what objects they signified; and after I had trained my mouth to form these signs, I used them to express my own desires. (*PI* §1; Augustine, *Confessions*, I. viii)

One might understand Wittgenstein's tale of the hurt child as a continuation of his contestation of Augustine's vision of language acquisition, a contestation begun with his counter-tale of the shopping trip in §1, and renewed pretty much whenever the figure of a child being taught recurs in the *Investigations* (which means, pretty much throughout the text). Of course, this point in Wittgenstein's investigation can be seen as one at which he acknowledges a deep insight in Augustine's account, to which his own is indebted; for his tale of pain also invokes the idea of a natural language of all peoples—a non-linguistic repertoire for the expression of inner moods, feelings, and the rest. But one could as easily see this as the point at which Wittgenstein acknowledges this debt by criticizing Augustine's way of invoking his insight; for Augustine places that insight in a context of assumptions that effectively work to undermine it.

To begin with, despite the fact that Augustine's child is presented as learning how to give expression to his desires, and to that extent to his inner experiences, what the world of his elders teaches him is essentially a set of public names for the objects upon which his desires are already directed. The clear implication is that the child is already capable of identifying what the objects of those desires, and hence the desires themselves, are; language is simply that which mediates between that internal moment of recognition and the public expression of the desires. Further, there is Augustine's uncanny suggestion that, in attaining such public expression, the child trains his mouth to form the relevant signs. This turn of phrase not only conjures up a vision of the child as the manipulative inhabitant of his own body, the master of a machine for speaking—as if at once puppet and puppeteer; it simultaneously underlines that the child is his own teacher (his elders pay him no heed), and that he effects the transition to linguistic expression not by anything like a process of substituting linguistic for non-linguistic expressive behaviour, but rather by setting up a naming relation between inner world and outer objects. The natural language of all peoples simply helps the child to establish that relation by and for himself, by functioning as a substitute for his elders' paying him any attention; their self-absorption is subverted or betrayed by the natural expressiveness of their bodies, rather than the natural expressiveness of the child's body being the means whereby they establish the relation for him, by establishing him within the human community of sufferers of pain.

If we press this comparison of Wittgenstein's child and Augustine's child a little further, two more points of contrast emerge. First, a partial explanation for Augustine's sense of the child as a tenant of its own body, as already possessed of a sophisticated inner world and hence as needing only a language with which to demand its public acknowledgement, lies in his evaluation of what one might call the spiritual status of the child. And Wittgenstein's way of emphasizing his contrary sense of the immediacy of his child's relation to his pain in §249 at once brings out and contests Augustine's spiritual agenda:

Are we perhaps over-hasty in our assumption that the smile of an unweaned infant is not a pretence?—And on what experience is our assumption based?

(Lying is a language-game that needs to be learned like any other one.) (*PI*, §249)

We shall return to the issue of pretence later in this discussion. But now, it is worth asking: why has Wittgenstein's child (*ein Kind*) become an unweaned infant (*eine Saugling*)? In part, without doubt, because he wishes to invoke a stage of human life so early that it has no room for the existence of certain relatively complex and necessarily intersubjective projects—no more room than exists in the life of the dog invoked in §250; the playing of such language-games must await the grafting of linguistic expressions upon a natural expressive repertoire that is inherently capable of accepting them, within the context of a complex social life. But his emphasis on the infant as unweaned, hence still at the breast, reminds us of a number of remarks that provide an immediate context in the *Confessions* for Augustine's self-taught, self-manipulating child[2]:

I have personally watched and studied a jealous baby. He could not yet speak and, pale with jealousy and bitterness, glared at his brother sharing his mother's milk. (*C*, I. vii)

When I did not get my way, either because I was not understood or lest it be harmful to me, I used to be indignant with my elders for their disobedience, and with free people who were not slaves to my interests; and I would revenge myself upon them by weeping. (*C*, I. vi)

By groans and various sounds and various movements of parts of my body I would endeavour to express the intentions of my heart to persuade people to bow to my will. (*C*, I. viii)

Augustine's child desires to find a means for the public expression of his desires so that he might bend others, and thereby the world, to his will; and that will—like the will of his elders, manifest in their apparently exclusive concern for having what they want and rejecting what is not in their interests—is itself fundamentally jealous, envious, and selfish. In short, for Augustine, the natural language of all peoples is that of original sin. And Wittgenstein means to invite us to ask: on what experience is Augustine's 'assumption' that his unweaned infant is consumed with bitter jealousy actually based?

The point here is not to suggest that the behaviour of unweaned infants cannot be seen in such a way. After all, the mother–child relation, as mediated through the breast, is a primary domain of psychoanalytic interpretation, and would certainly be seen as host

---

[2] I am using Henry Chadwick's translation of Augustine's *Confessions* (Oxford: Oxford University Press, 1991); hereafter *C*.

to (necessarily primitive versions of) jealousy, envy, and hatred. But the tales of infant life engendered by psychoanalysis are grounded in the world of adult experience—in how the expressive life of adults has been found to be subject to neurotic, psychotic, and other forms of suffering, and how attempts properly to acknowledge and redirect such patterns of thought, word, and deed have been found to call for a certain interpretation of the life of the unweaned infant.

In this respect, Augustine's interpretation of the child as originally sinful is on all fours with Freud's interpretation of the child as working to establish boundaries around and within the self by at once rejecting and internalizing aspects of its mother and father. We understand children in the terms made available by our understanding of adults, or elders—call them grown-ups (*Erwachsenen*), those we think of as having put away childish things without ever leaving them entirely behind, because we can find no better way of understanding their adult ways. And this suggests a further sense in which the child's acquisition of language, and hence accession to human maturity, might be thought of as constituted by an intervention from the very social world that he can and must come to inhabit. For if that acquisition depends upon his elders' ability and willingness to see his behaviour as expressive (as the natural, primitive manifestation) of human moods, feelings, sensations, and the rest, it will be pervasively determined by their (which means their and his society's) conception of what genuinely human moods, feelings, sensations, and the rest are and should be—a conception that is always already manifest in what those elders say and do (for example, in the fact that lying is one of the things they habitually do with their words).

One might think of this as a point at which Wittgenstein's thought makes contact with Girard's idea of human identity as mimetic.[3] According to Girard, human beings become individuals

[3] For more on this theme, see sect. 12 of the 'Concluding Dogmatic Postscript' to my *Inheritance and Originality*.

by incorporating gestures, language, modes of consciousness, and activity from those around them; this mimicry or incorporation of the other is not something selves do, but rather what makes the human animal a bearer of selfhood in the first place. Consequently, human desire is not linear (a matter of subjects fixing directly upon objects) or reflexive (a matter of desiring another's desire, wanting the other to find oneself desirable), but rather triangular, or mediated (we desire what another desires, according to the desire of the other). And for Girard, this mimetic structure of selfhood secretes rivalry, conflict, and lethal violence in so far as it engenders individuals who each desire what the other desires in a domain of finite resources. One might even think that the interpretations of childhood offered by Augustine and Freud are interpretations of whatever it is about the human animal that is the subject of Girard's interpretation.

Whatever the merits of this suggestion, however, it is plain that Wittgenstein's child will take in a certain (that is, not one particular, but rather some, more or less particular) understanding of what it is to have an inner life, and of what such lives contain, along with his mother's milk. The graft of language and the graft of a particular understanding of what it is to be human are jointly effected in these exchanges between the crying child and its elders. In this sense, the child not only suffers pain; even when that pain is self-inflicted, and thus not the result of another's actions (perhaps actions of blame and punishment), in coming to understand that this is what it is suffering, it suffers the implantation or introjection of language and society.

But I mentioned a second detail that is made salient if we compare Wittgenstein's suffering child and Augustine's learner. We have already noted that, whereas Augustine's elders make no attempt to teach the child in their midst, and thereby place their child in the position of one who has to help himself to their words (even steal them), Wittgenstein's elders do respond to the crying child; they take on the responsibility of teachers, and he learns something from them. However, against the background of a point Wittgenstein makes much later, the mode or limits of that response can seem almost as bizarre as that of Augustine's elders.

What sort of issue is: Is it the *body* that feels pain?—How is it to be decided? What makes it plausible to say that it is *not* the body?—Well, something like this: if someone has a pain in his hand, then the hand does not say so (unless it writes it) and one does not comfort the hand, but the sufferer: one looks into his face.

How am I filled with pity *for this man?* How does it come out what the object of my pity is? (Pity, one may say, is a form of conviction that someone else is in pain.) (*PI*, §§286–7)

When Wittgenstein's child hurts himself and cries, his elders talk to him and teach him exclamations and words; they do not do what any ordinary grown-up would surely do in such a situation, and that, Wittgenstein implies, is just as significant in constituting our sense of the nature of pain (by helping to constitute our sense that pain is not just a fact about another to be noted, but a condition to be acknowledged)—namely, comfort the child, offer him some form of sympathetic response (perhaps pity, perhaps encouragement) to the fact that he is in pain. If the problem with Augustine's elders is that they refuse the role of teachers, the problem with Wittgenstein's elders is that they refuse to transcend that role: they seem to look upon their child's suffering solely as an opportunity for education, as if their concern for him extended exclusively to his prospects as a fellow-speaker.

But perhaps this apparent limitation in their response should be understood otherwise. For we could interpret their provision of exclamations and then sentences not as an alternative to offering comfort, but as their way of offering comfort. In other words, we might think of the provision of a language for pain to someone immersed in inarticulate suffering as a means of giving him some perspective on his own condition—at least enough distance from it to articulate that condition, and thereby to place him in the position of acknowledging the state he is in, which must include acknowledging that it may end, that he may be comforted, that he might transcend that state, if only in his imagination. One might in fact think that, precisely in so far as the acquisition of a language for pain (and indeed for any of our moods, feelings, and the rest) places us in the realm of common discourse and the intersubjective relations with which it is interwoven, it displaces us from a position in which, in so far as what one is feeling is as nothing to others, it is nothing less than everything to us—a way in which our identity is overwhelmed by the particular state we happen to be in.[4] Here, then, is a sense in which we might coherently seek, and see point in seeking, to use language to get between pain and its (immediate, all-encompassing) expression.

We might go one step further. For if it is the introjection of language and society that makes it possible for the child to avoid being lost in, and hence to, his experience, if without that internalization he would lack the capacity to articulate and hence acknowledge the state he is in, then it becomes tempting to say that the child's achievement of self-awareness and selfhood here appears as a matter of achieving a certain kind of internal self-differentiation. In internalizing his elders' gift of language, he internalizes (its and their) otherness: he gains the capacity to distance himself from himself, to achieve a perspective on his own condition—which means acknowledging that his present condition is never all that there is to him, that there is in addition the relation in which he necessarily stands to that condition, the specific mode of his acknowledgement or denial of it. Sartre would say that we are here touching on the self's necessary failure to coincide with itself, its not being what it is and its being what it is not; Heidegger would call it the self's uncanniness, its necessary transcendence of, or projection beyond, its present situation. In the terms provided by Wittgenstein's tale, we might say that what the child acquires from

[4] This thought is central to Elaine Scarry's fascinating account of pain in relation to torture, war, politics, and religion in *The Body in Pain* (Cambridge, Mass.: Harvard University Press, 1985).

his elders is not just the meaning of 'pain' (and so the significance of pain), but the meaning or significance of language and society as such—its gift of otherness to oneself.

Is this why Wittgenstein's child is said to have hurt himself (rather than being hurt by others)? For that small detail in this primal scene suggests a solipsistic self-relation that seems, as it were, too immediate to make room for genuine selfhood, the experience eliciting a cry that no one—not even the one crying—can really hear or respond to, say acknowledge. However, once the circle widens sufficiently for acknowledgement by others and by the child himself to be possible, the fact that this is achieved by the introduction of new pain behaviour in the place of that original cry further implies that what is thereby brought to acknowledgement is not just this child's pain but the inherently painful nature of the individual's entry into the human form of life with language. It is quite as if the necessary internalization of otherness is not merely to be suffered—something given to the infant, with respect to which it is passive—but is also itself painful or traumatic, as if the attainment of selfhood in a society of words is a kind of self-harm (or at least, that it is always imagined or fantasized after the event in such terms—as a loss of paradisal self-sufficiency, of an immediacy to oneself that is in reality incompatible with genuine selfhood).

In exploring all these complexities, however, we have omitted to account for one puzzling feature of Wittgenstein's tale of the crying child, and of the moral he means us to draw from it: the fact that the whole they constitute (all three sentences of it) is introduced as 'one possibility'. Given the importance Wittgenstein attaches to the connection between non-linguistic and linguistic expressive behaviour, how can he allow himself to present it simply as one possibility (presumably, one amongst others)? Does this mean that he thinks that natural expressive behaviour and verbal expressions might conceivably be otherwise connected—even that they might not be so connected in actual, everyday human life? If so, how can the possible connection he envisages deliver the essence of the matter, with respect to sensations or to any other psychological phenomenon? If not, why not simply assert that what he claims is in fact the case?

Here, we need to note that Wittgenstein's tale, with its moral, is a response to his interlocutor; and we have already noted that this interlocutor's question is one about the sheer possibility of talk about sensations. He does not question the fact that we do have a life with sensation-words; what he questions is *how* we do—how we could so much as make a connection of any kind between sensations and the names we undeniably have for them. Hence, the assertion of facts as facts can do nothing to assuage such an anxiety; but by the same token, all that is necessary to overcome it altogether is the interlocutor's acknowledgement that it is at least a possibility that things might be thus-and-so.

It is also worth pointing out that the interlocutor's question is being responded to in its reformulated and reinterpreted form—that is, as a question about how a human being learns the meaning of the names of sensations. Hence, the form in which Wittgenstein states his position is that of an answer to that question—that is, as a claim about how sensation-words are acquired. And the moral he wishes us to draw from this answer is one concerning the way in which sensation-words function—the way in which they are used and interwoven with our broader life with language. Hence, the interest of his claim about how they are acquired is meant to reside primarily in the light this claim casts on the mode in which the acquired words are used. Hence, he could happily allow that the words are in fact mastered in other ways, as long as we accept that they could have been so mastered, and hence that what is mastered is necessarily consonant with that possibility.

In fact, as we shall see, it is not long before Wittgenstein explicitly allows that sensation-words might be acquired in other ways. For in §257, he responds with apparent impatience to the thought that we can dismiss the very idea of a private language by pointing out that it would be impossible to teach a child who showed no outwards signs of pain the use of the word 'tooth-ache': 'Well, let's assume the child is a genius and itself invents a name for the sensation!' Of course, he quickly goes on to test the putative significance of pretty much every word in that characterization; but the philosophical dialectic that he thereby induces would be utterly pointless if he is not prepared at least to contemplate the thought that things might be otherwise than they are, and in ways that cannot be settled a priori. Hence, he cannot place decisive weight at this point on the claim that things in fact are as he says they might be with respect to acquiring sensation-words; but then, neither does he need to put any such weight upon them. So he doesn't.

3

Wittgenstein's Cloud: Of Unknowing (§246)

In §243, the idea of a private language was characterized as a body of words referring to its speaker's immediate private sensations. If we think of §244 as interrogating the sense of the term 'reference' in this context, and of §245 as doing the same for the companion idea of 'immediate' (that is, for the idea that our access to our own inner experiences is not mediated by anything), then §246 begins to interrogate the conception of sensations as 'private'.

In what sense are my sensations *private?*—Well, only I can know whether I am really in pain; another person can only surmise it.—In one way this is wrong, and in another nonsense. If we are using the word 'to know' as it is normally used (and how else are we to use it?), then other people very often know when I am in pain.—Yes, but all the same not with the certainty with which I know it myself!—It can't be said of me at all (except perhaps as a joke) that I *know* I am in pain. What is it supposed to mean—except perhaps that I *am* in pain?

Other people cannot be said to learn of my sensations *only* from my behaviour,—for *I* cannot be said to learn of them. I *have* them.

The truth is: it makes sense to say about other people that they doubt whether I am in pain; but not to say it about myself. (*PI* §246)

A resolute reader can happily acknowledge the essential responsiveness of Wittgenstein's stance in these paragraphs; their author begins by asking a question, and what follows is essentially reactive to the answer to that question provided by his interlocutor. But a substantial reader would be quick to point out that the mode or tone of that response is not exactly open-minded, on the face of it. For the interlocutor's words are hardly out of his mouth before they are roundly condemned as a synthesis of falsehood and nonsensicality. The point here is not so much that Wittgenstein's response returns us to certain articulations of grammar—as we noted earlier, both resolute and substantial readings surely require such moments of normativity. What should disturb the resolute reader, rather, is the way in which Wittgenstein prepares that return. For here, he seems essentially uninterested in the possibility of any unclarity or ambiguity in what his interlocutor might mean by his answer to the opening question; he does not ask himself, and thereby invite us to ask ourselves, what the interlocutor might be trying to get at through his invocation of a cognitive disparity between the first-person and third-person cases. Instead, he responds as if the meanings of the words he employs are either self-evident and singular (adverting to *the* normal use of the word 'to know'), or barely capable of an alternative interpretation ('except perhaps as a joke'). This apparent refusal to open himself to other possibilities of sense is epitomized by the moment when he turns words which might have been used to invite an exercise of the sympathetic imagination to purely sarcastic intent ('How else are we to use it?', 'What is it supposed to mean?'). And without allowing such space for the imagination to be exercised, there seems to be little ground for attributing a resolute strategy to Wittgenstein at this point.

An immediate response available to the resolute reader is to point to the second paragraph of §246. For Wittgenstein's exactingly compact opening sentence first presents us with the denial of an assertion that seems just obviously true—as if it were simply reminding us that what we say and do typically reveals our pain to others; then it points out that the presence of the little word 'only' implies a contrast between routes or modes of learning, and so between the person in pain and those observing him, that simply has no purchase in this context (since the 'owner' of a pain does not learn that he is in pain in some way other than that of observing his own behaviour); but if the 'only' is to that extent empty or idling, then so is the apparently truistic assertion that contains it. The concision of this revelation should not make it any less disturbing; for it reveals that even (or especially?) when the truth of an utterance seems most fully or wholly obvious, its meaning can nevertheless be essentially undetermined. Here, the resolute moral consists not only in the lesson that not even the smallest, most unassuming word can be left to fend for itself in philosophy, but in the disparity between the factor that causes the trouble and the trouble it causes; and the speed with which Wittgenstein pulls the rug from under our feet here dramatizes the completeness with which such apparently minor matters can lay us low.

But this kind of reading of the second paragraph does not directly address the difficulties raised by the first; and here we can begin to broach Stanley Cavell's distinctive treatment of Wittgenstein's remarks on private languages, which received its first public airing in the penultimate essay of *Must We Mean What We Say?* This essay, entitled 'Knowing and Acknowledging', takes as its foil the far more familiar understanding of Wittgenstein's stance developed by Norman Malcolm.[1] With respect to §246, Malcolm feels justified in concluding that 'I know I'm in pain' is straightforwardly senseless; as he puts it, the 'I know' in such a context 'cannot do any of its normal jobs'—those jobs being the claiming of grounds, of authority, and of privileged knowledge. He grounds his own authority to make these claims by reminding us, amongst other things, of the fact that expressions of doubt and attempts to cite evidence in such first-person cases would be

---

[1] N. Malcolm, 'The Privacy of Experience', in A. Stroll (ed.), *Epistemology* (New York: Harper & Row, 1967); Cavell, *Must We Mean What We Say?* (New York: Cambridge University Press, 1969), hereafter *MWM*.

misplaced, and concludes that so—to the same extent—must be claims to knowledge.

Cavell's response is to ask whether there are no other relevant functions of 'I know'.

Here are three more: (1) There is 'I know New York (Sanskrit, the signs of the Zodiac, Greta Garbo, myself).' To know in such cases is to have become acquainted with, or to have learned, or got the hang of. (2) There is, again, 'I know I am a nuisance', 'I know I am being childish', 'I know I am late'. To (say you) know in these cases is to admit, confess, *acknowledge*. (3) There is, again, the use of 'I know' to *agree* or confirm what has been said, or to say I *already* knew.—Can it be shown that none of these additional uses exemplifies a (the) relevant use of 'I know' in 'I know I'm in pain'? (*MWM* 255)

The existence of these other, perfectly ordinary uses of 'I know' in first-person cases first of all highlights the fact that Malcolm's supposedly exhaustive list of three normal uses of that phrase in fact concentrates exclusively on those which are connected with the idea of certainty—uses where it contrasts with 'I believe', where it involves claiming that one is in a distinctive position to know something, and where one must be able to document or otherwise ground that claim. And this fact about Malcolm should return us to the words of §246, where the sceptic's defence of his initial answer to Wittgenstein's opening question reveals that he is making exactly the same connection between 'I know' and certainty ('. . . not with the certainty with which I know it myself!'). Malcolm wishes, quite rightly in Cavell's view, to deny that first-person expressions of pain have the function of claiming certainty; but he does so by denying that 'I know I'm in pain' has any use in such contexts, and this strategy implicitly accepts the sceptic's assumption that 'I know' has no significant use except in association with claims to certainty. Malcolm's inability to question this assumption, an aspect of his blindness to the real varieties of normal use of 'I know' in first-person contexts, accordingly entails that his contestation of the sceptic amounts to a further expression of scepticism.

We shall return to the first of Cavell's three additional uses of 'know' in a moment; but it is worth allowing him to spell out a little further what he means to include within the second such use, the one he captures by means of his signature concept of 'acknowledgement', which he introduces in the context of third-person rather than first-person claims about pain. In essence, that concept incorporates Wittgenstein's sense (glanced at a little earlier, and evident in §286–7) that another's pain is not simply a further fact about them (to be noted or overlooked, or seen to be beyond the metaphysical range of any gaze of ours, as the case may be), but rather a condition of theirs that requires a response from me.

[Y]our suffering makes a *claim* upon me. It is not enough that I *know* (am certain) that you suffer—I must do or reveal something (whatever can be done). In a word, I must *acknowledge* it, otherwise I do not know what 'your (your or his) being in pain' means. . . . But obviously sympathy may not be forthcoming. So when I say that 'We must acknowledge one another's suffering, and we do that by responding to a claim upon our sympathy', I do not mean that we always in fact *have* sympathy, nor that we always ought to have it. The claim of suffering may go unanswered. We may feel lots of things—sympathy, *Schadenfreude*, nothing. If one says that this is a *failure* to acknowledge another's suffering, surely this would not mean that we fail, in such cases, to *know* that he is suffering? We may or may not. The point, however, is that the concept of acknowledgement is evidenced equally by its failure as by its success. It is not a description of a given response but a category in terms of which a given response is evaluated. . . . A 'failure to know' might just mean a piece of ignorance, an absence of something, a blank. A 'failure to acknowledge' is the presence of something, a confusion, an indifference, a callousness, an exhaustion, a coldness. Spiritual emptiness is not a blank. (*MWM* 263–4)

On such a reading of Wittgenstein's response to the second clause of the sceptic's opening claim ('another can only surmise [whether or not I am in pain]'), the impatience that is given expression in his counter-claim that others very often know when I am in pain is not directed at the falseness of the sceptic's view, but rather at the terms within which it assumes that the debate must be conducted. For when knowledge is yoked to certainty, it takes on a primarily, even an exclusively, epistemic cast: it pictures the other's pain as an empirical presence or absence, a state of affairs in the world about which we might be ignorant or well-informed, and that consequently raises questions solely about our cognitive reach. That is indeed *a* normal use of the concept of 'knowledge'—a use that both grounds and subverts more general sceptical questions about knowledge of 'the external world'; but is it *the* normal use of that concept in conjunction with the concept of pain?

Pains are not independently given features of the world: if there is a pain in the world, then I am in pain, or you are, or she is (or some sentient creature is); and any person in pain wants others to know of it (or to fail to know of it) because those others will respond (or fail to respond) to that knowledge in some way. To identify another as in pain is not simply or merely or just to make a claim about that portion of the world; it is to identify something about that other as making a claim on me (which I may or may not acknowledge). Hence, even to establish that one *can* know that another is in pain (by reminding us that we do often claim or act upon such knowledge) is not a way of making progress against the sceptic; for without an examination of *what* one knows (of what the concept of knowledge signifies) in such cases, nothing in particular has been established thereby. Indeed, being preoccupied with establishing this point in this way would amount to colluding with the sceptic's conflation of one use of the concept of knowledge with another, and hence with his simultaneous transformation and reversal of the fundamental claiming relation here—his occlusion of the other's actual human claim upon me by my putative cognitive claim upon the other. Wittgenstein's impatience is thus an attempt to clear the way for a more patient evaluation of what knowing another's pain actually, normally means—for a proper acknowledgement of our answerability to another's suffering.

According to Cavell, however, the concept of acknowledgement brings out essential aspects of our use of the concept of knowledge in first-person as well as (second- and) third-person cases; and here we return directly to the second of the three uses of 'I know' that he offers to Malcolm. By emphasizing this, Cavell aims to bring us to see that the concept of acknowledgement might not only contest the sceptic's position; it might also provide a better way of articulating what the sceptic is actually, and rightly, responding to in adopting his position. Suppose, for example, that the sceptic were to say, 'Only he can acknowledge his pain; I can't'; how would this differ from saying, 'Only he can know whether he's in pain; I can't'? For Cavell, being in a position to acknowledge something is hardly weaker than being in a position to know something:

On the contrary: from my acknowledging that I am late it follows that I know I'm late (which is what my words say); but from my knowing I am late, it does not follow that I acknowledge that I'm late—otherwise, human relationships would be altogether other than they are. One could say: Acknowledgement goes beyond knowledge. (Goes beyond not, so to speak, in the order of knowledge, but in its requirement that I *do* something or reveal something on the basis of that knowledge.)

Is it, then, a suppressed premise of the sceptic's that 'If he can acknowledge he's in pain, then he knows whether he is in pain'? And would we deny this premise?—'Still, this does not alter the fact that if he says "I know I'm in pain" he will not be expressing certainty and *this* is what the sceptic needs.'—Perhaps he will not be expressing *certainty*; but why can one not say, what his words say, that he is expressing *knowledge*? (*MWM* 257)

In other words, even if the sceptic is wrong to equate expressions of knowledge in the first-person case with expressions of certainty, he is not wrong in sensing that there is such a thing as expression of knowledge in the first-person case—because there can be such a thing as acknowledging that one is in pain, and the concept of acknowledgement includes the concept of knowledge. He is thus right to insist that if a person is in pain, then she knows that she is—for this would then mean that she can acknowledge that she is; but since something that can be acknowledged can also be denied (since acknowledgement is not a description of a given response, but a category in terms of which responses can be evaluated), this insistence might also be seen to register the fact that we will not know that another person is in pain unless she acknowledges it—that is, unless it finds expression in what she says and does (sometimes, despite her best efforts to suppress it).

In short, the truth underlying the sceptical impulse here is the one we first encountered in §244, that a person's behaviour is expressive of her mind; and this truth has, so to speak, two aspects. It entails that our knowledge of another's feelings is dependent upon her giving expression to them in what she says and does, whereas her knowledge of them is not; and it also implies that there may be ways in which she can fail to acknowledge her feelings not only to us but to herself, and hence ways in which she might fail to know her own feelings.

The first aspect of the situation is that to which the sceptic gives erroneous expression when she insists that the person in pain is certain that she is in pain; the truth of the matter is that she is not free not to know her pain, that she is impaled upon her knowledge because she is impaled upon her pain—and we are not. This, one might say, is an aspect of our separateness, of the fact that her position is not mine, that I am not her. And this facet of the human condition does, as the sceptic insists, bring in its train certain special problems about knowledge when it is knowledge of another that we seek, even if the sceptic wrongly characterizes what these special problems are. They are not problems of fallibility or openness to doubt (which concern our epistemic reach regardless of what we seek to know—whether another's pains or the numbers of pots and pans in her kitchen), or a constitutive metaphysical ignorance effected by the barrier of the other's body; they relate, rather, to the responsibilities engendered by (on the one hand) the other person's ability and willingness to suppress or misrepresent—as well as to express—what she cannot fail to feel, and (on the other) our ability and willingness to identify and respond to her expressions, suppressions, and misrepresentations.

The second aspect of the truth in scepticism is not one to which the sceptic appears to be any more sensitive than his opponents. Cavell expresses it as follows:

[T]o say that behaviour is expressive is not to say that the man impaled upon his sensation must express it in his behaviour; it is to say that in order not to express it he must *suppress* the behaviour, or twist it. And if he twists it far or often enough, he may lose possession of the region of the mind which that behaviour is expressing. (*MWM*, 264)

This last claim may not seem plausible with the example of pain in the forefront of our attention; but that may simply mark the point at which this choice of example can occlude the specific nature of other mental phenomena, and hence distort our thinking about knowing oneself more generally. Pain is a phenomenon fully transparent to consciousness; it finds expression in more or less definite forms of behaviour; and it seems particularly easy to draw a distinction between inner and outer with respect to it. Other mental phenomena—such as envy, or a sense of loss, or ringing in one's ears, and others (for example, grief or despair) which may themselves be painful—lack one or another of these features, and any grammatical investigation which was led by them would explore rather different kinds of relationship in which we might stand to them.

In *The Claim of Reason*, Cavell cites a passage from Wittgenstein that, in his view, appears to generalize the lessons of pain too quickly: 'It is correct to say "I know what you are thinking", and wrong to say "I know what I am thinking". (A whole cloud of philosophy condensed into a drop of grammar)' (*PI* p. 222).

I find this much less convincing; I'm still under a cloud. I sort of know what it means: it is not merely that I do not have to look at myself to see or to learn whether I am thinking; but that I do not, as it were, take stock of the contents of my mind and determine whether they are in there. And yet it would be correct to say: 'What you say keeps not ringing true to me. I keep having this worry—I can't quite put my finger on what it is.—Ah, yes, I have it, I know what I am thinking . . .'. It is still true that saying

'I know' here doesn't contrast with 'I believe' or 'I doubt'. But doesn't it contrast with 'I don't know' or 'can't tell' or 'can't make it out'?...

And when it comes to regions of the soul like envy or charity or ambition or self-destructiveness, or coldness covered with affectionateness, or loneliness covered with activity, or hatred covered by judiciousness, or obsessiveness covered by intellectuality...one's lack of knowledge of oneself may fully contrast with one's beliefs about oneself. My condition then is not that I need no criteria for such states, but that I fail accurately to allow of myself the ones I have. And here my relation to myself is expressed by saying that I do not know myself. (*CR* 101)

One might say that what goes missing in Wittgenstein's remark is the first of the three alternative uses of 'I know' that Cavell cites in response to Malcolm—that of becoming acquainted with, or getting the hang of, oneself. But how far does this highly local disagreement extend to Wittgenstein's more general conception of the asymmetries between first-person and third-person uses of psychological concepts? What does Cavell mean when he talks, in these first-person cases, of allowing myself the criteria that I have? Take the example of someone claiming that she is expecting someone or something. There may well be feelings which go with the concentration, anticipation, release, and so on involved in such cases, and their presence may lead her to say that she is expecting something; but whether they do or not will depend upon the circumstances in which they occur. It will, for example, matter whether she has them whilst laying the table for a dinner party, or when washing up after it; and what would make them 'queer' in the latter case would not be anything intrinsic to them, but rather their inappropriateness to the context—when there is nothing in the circumstances to be expected.

If it is true that the having of my feelings *alone* cannot make possible my knowledge of myself ..., this says something about the nature of self-knowledge; that it depends upon my knowing or appreciating the place or reach—I want to say, the normality or abnormality—of those feelings to the situation in which those feelings occur.... Knowing oneself is the capacity, as I wish to put it, for placing-oneself-in-the-world. It is not merely that to know I have in fact *done* what I intended. . . . I have to look to see *whether* it is done; it is also, and crucially, that I have to know that *that* circumstance is (counts as) what I did. (*CR* 107–8]

On Cavell's account, my use of criteria in the first-person case is not to establish what I am feeling, or to establish that it is I who feel it; it is to establish that these feelings in these circumstances add up to expectation (as opposed to some other state). In so doing, I use the same criteria here that others would use in judging whether I am expecting something, although I do not use them in the same way—not on the basis of observation of their presence or fulfilment.

Since this picture of self-knowledge, and the role of criteria within it, explicitly avoids yoking the concept of knowledge in the first-person case to that of certainty, Wittgenstein's brusquely critical response to his interlocutor's assumption of just such a yoke in §246 need not give us any reason to think that he would reject Cavell's way with these words. But to what extent is Cavell able to endorse Wittgenstein's way with the words of his sceptical interlocutor in that section? How far does his critique of Malcolm's reading of Wittgenstein apply also to Wittgenstein himself? This will depend upon how far we take Wittgenstein's words to commit him to the assumption that both the sceptical interlocutor and Malcolm share—that the use of 'I know' to indicate certainty exhausts the possible range of its uses in these first-person contexts.

I have already suggested that several turns of phrase in his first paragraph speak against the thought that Wittgenstein is either plainly aware of those alternative, non-epistemic uses of 'I know', or concerned to open up the possibility that something real and important lies behind the interlocutor's misbegotten ways of articulating his conception of privacy—namely, his sarcastic rather than inviting uses of the questions 'how else are we to use it?' and 'What is it supposed to mean?'. The countervailing force of the fact that he does canvass the possibility of using 'I know' as a joke is thus undermined at least to some extent, not only by its own hesitancy, but also by the general rhetorical register that these questions establish and epitomize.

Nevertheless, two factors speak in favour of the thought that Wittgenstein does not commit himself to the assumption that knowledge is a matter of certainty, and both are significant precisely because of the primary formal fact about the paragraph that is so significant to the resolute reader of Wittgenstein's text—that it is presented exclusively as a response to the words of his interlocutor. For it is the interlocutor who directs our attention to the specific example of pain in his initial response to Wittgenstein's opening question, and who makes fully explicit in his second contribution to the dialogue his assumption that to talk of knowing in this context is to talk of certainty. If, then, we regard it as central to Wittgenstein's later conception of philosophy that he adopt a purely responsive role in his dialogues with his interlocutors (just as he claims in the *Tractatus* that it is central to any strictly correct method in philosophy that one say nothing oneself, and instead restrict oneself to indicating to those who do say something when they have given no meaning to one of the words of their utterance—*Tractatus*, 6.53), then we might read his remarks in this paragraph as wholly negative in intent. The interpretative proposal here is as follows: *if* the feeling we are concerned with is pain, and *if* by 'knowing' we mean certainty, then what the interlocutor is saying about knowing his own pain stands in need of a variety of decisive corrections. There may be other feelings and states of mind to consider, and other ways of using 'I know' in the first person to canvass; but these are irrelevant to the particular interlocutory dialogue presently under way, and may anyway be better grasped when the assumptions behind this exchange are entirely uprooted.

One further point in support of such a resolute reading of §246 might emerge from a more careful examination of the precise terms in which the interlocutor articulates his yoking of knowledge and certainty. In his initial remark, he says that one person 'can only surmise' that another is in pain; the German term translated as 'surmise' is *vermuten*—which invokes the idea of a supposition or assumption, and at the limit that of (sheer?) speculation or guesswork, and contains the factor *mut*, which means courage or bravery. In his second remark, he invokes the idea of 'certainty', which translates the German word *Sicherheit*; this also carries connotations of security or safety. In short, the interlocutor's words suggest not only an epistemic gloss on the concept of knowledge, but also a certain emotional or evaluative dimension to interpersonal relations; it is as if coming to know another's pain amounts to making a bold leap beyond our cognitive limits, whereas knowing one's own pain is guaranteed to be effortless.

Perhaps, then, the brusqueness and banked fire of Wittgenstein's responses to this interlocutor are engendered not solely by his conflation of knowledge with certainty, but also by his implication that knowledge of others requires exceptional daring, whereas knowledge of oneself is automatic. For if anything like Cavell's picture of these matters is right, then, whilst knowing others may ask of us the courage to admit our tendency to deny or overlook their thoughts and feelings, knowing ourselves is never a mechanical deliverance. And this inversion of the truth would be particularly galling to an author whose philosophical investigations into what we say when are themselves exercises in self-knowledge, and unduly arduous (even painful) ones at that.

4

Privacy, Patience, and Pictures: First Methodological Interlude (§§248, 251–2)

The proposition "Sensations are private" is comparable to: "One plays patience by oneself". . . .

What does it mean when we say: "I can't imagine the opposite of this" or "What would it be like, if it were otherwise?"—For example, when someone has said that my images are private, or that only I myself can know whether I am feeling pain, and similar things.

Of course, here "I can't imagine the opposite" doesn't mean: my powers of imagination are unequal to the task. These words are a defence against something whose form makes it look like an empirical proposition, but which is really a grammatical one.

But why do we say: "I can't imagine the opposite"? Why not: "I can't imagine the thing itself"?

Example: "Every rod has a length". That means something like: we call something (or *this*) "the length of a rod"—but nothing "the length of a sphere". Now can I imagine "every rod having a length"? Well, I simply imagine a rod. Only this picture, in connexion with this proposition, has a quite different role from one used in connexion with the proposition "This table has the same length as the one over there". For here I understand what it means to have a picture of the opposite (nor need it be a mental picture).

But the picture attaching to the grammatical proposition could only show, say, what is called "the length of a rod". And what should the opposite picture be?

((Remark about the negation of an a priori proposition.))

"This body has extension." To this we might reply: "Nonsense!"—but are inclined to reply "Of course!"—Why is this? (*PI* §§248, 251–2)

The internal structure of this (interrupted) reflection on the status of the conclusions established in §246 is complex. First, Wittgenstein offers two pairs of propositions that he explicitly claims (or implies) are comparable with each other: first, 'Sensations are private' and 'One plays patience by oneself', and then 'Every rod has a length' and 'This body has extension'. Their comparability resides in their tendency to elicit the following kind of response from those to whom they are addressed: 'I can't imagine the opposite', or 'What would it be like if it were otherwise?' Wittgenstein suggests (call this the second level of his reflections) that this betrays an implicit awareness on the part of the respondents that these pairs of propositions are grammatical rather than empirical—by which he means that they do not represent a state of affairs that might have been otherwise, but would rather be advanced (to quote the preceding §247) 'when one was explaining the meaning of the word ['sensation', or 'patience', or 'rod' or 'body'] to him. For then it means: *that* is how we use it.' He illustrates this distinction by replacing invocations of the imagination with an imaginary invocation of the different ways in which one might use pictures (whether mental or physical) in the two kinds of case. And the same imaginative exercise provides us with a way of answering a further question, namely: Why do we respond to such grammatical remarks by saying 'Of course!' rather than by saying 'Nonsense!' (call this the third level of Wittgenstein's reflections)? To which his suggested answer seems to be: because, in such cases, any representation of the phenomenon under consideration would (it seems) depict it as having the relevant property, we simply do not understand what it might mean to have a picture of the opposite (that is, of that phenomenon lacking that property). But then it is bound to seem that we can (indeed, that we can only) imagine the thing itself—that any imaginable rod will of course have a length, as any body will have extension. How, then, we might plausibly think, could it be nonsensical to say so?

There is a certain aptness in the transition here from a grammatical investigation of our uses of psychological concepts to a grammatical investigation of the difference between grammatical and empirical remarks (and hence, of philosophical method as it finds expression in such investigations). For on Wittgenstein's conception of the matter, philosophical dialogue is always therapeutic in its purposes; hence, it is concerned with understanding the complex of desires, intentions, fantasies, and confusions that find expression in the interlocutor's contribution to such dialogues. Hence, our involvement in such dialogues necessarily involves us in a mode of psychological understanding (of others, and of ourselves in so far as the interlocutor expresses our own compulsions and convictions); so when a philosophical dialogue focuses on the grammar of psychological concepts, it is in effect a study of one of its own most central resources. Hence, each step within it can invite a transition to such reflexive levels of reflection.

Wittgenstein's use of the example of a rod when exploring that second level of reflection here (that is, when asking what it is for something to be a grammatical as opposed to an empirical matter) seems equally, if more specifically, apt. For, with its connotation of a measuring rod or ruler (a suggestion reinforced by Wittgenstein's association of the rod's length with the question of a table's length, quite as if the former were a means of ascertaining the latter), we are reminded thereby of his earlier discussion of the standard metre—that bar or rod in the Louvre which functioned as the final court of appeal in the system of metric measurement. When Wittgenstein suggests (in §50) that the standard metre is the one thing of which we can say neither that it is, nor that it is not, one metre long, he characterizes that as marking its peculiar role in the language-game of measuring with a metre-rule. For if we were to try to represent its length as being one metre, and someone were to ask us what we meant by 'one metre', we could only point to the bar itself—thereby implying that what we had claimed amounted only to the empty 'assertion' that 'this bar is as long as it is'.

In other words, Wittgenstein's suggestion reflects the fact that the standard metre is an instrument of that dimension of our language of measurement; in the system of metric measurement, it is a means of representation rather than something that is represented. Hence, in so far as one can intelligibly remark that 'the standard metre is one metre long', that remark will function as an explanation of what we mean by 'one metre' (or perhaps as an explanation of what we mean by 'standard metre'); it will, in other words, clarify the meaning of a word rather than conveying any information about the length of that particular rod or bar. It will, in short, be a grammatical proposition—which is exactly the status Wittgenstein is here assigning explicitly to the remark that 'every rod has a length' (as opposed to 'this table is the same length as that one'), and implicitly to the remark that 'sensations are private'.

With that contrast in mind, however, and prompted by Wittgenstein's decision to examine questions of meaningfulness by way of pictures and depiction (as if inviting us to remember the *Tractatus*), we might recall our task of evaluating the relative merits of substantial and resolute readings of this text. It then becomes striking that the concluding reiteration of Wittgenstein's third level of discussion (in §252) implies that one might perfectly legitimately respond to an example of what he has been characterizing as a grammatical proposition as if it were a piece of nonsense. In other words, the signature gesture of Wittgenstein's later philosophical method, itself avowedly designed to show us that we have fallen into emptiness in our speech, can itself be seen as trading or participating in—one might call it acting out—the very same emptiness. Why?

We can find the beginning of an answer by noting that what elicits this characterization of grammatical remarks as nonsense is our prior inclination to characterize them as obvious or a matter of course—as something that could not be otherwise. As the opening exchanges of §251 dramatize the process, we try to defend ourselves against claims which appear to be empirical by saying that we can't imagine the opposite. But this could easily suggest that we have a clear idea of what it is that we cannot imagine—something we refer to as 'the opposite' of our interlocutor's claim concerning the privacy of images or sensations, a specific possibility that we claim lies beyond our imaginative or conceptual grasp. And this in turn suggests that grammar is excluding or prohibiting us from something in particular—that the limit at issue is in fact a limitation. In other words, even though we mean simply to be saying that this 'something' is not a genuine possibility, the way in which we do so actually subverts its purpose by implying that we can grasp that impossibility in thought, and hence that it is in reality a peculiar kind of possibility—the kind excluded by grammar. In so doing, we fall victim to the very emptiness we are attempting to criticize.

By the same token, if we say (in response to an implicitly grammatical remark masquerading as an empirical one) that we can't imagine the opposite, we might seem to imply that the opposite of that opposite is something that we can imagine, that we can (as it were) imagine the thing itself, that which the grammatical remark articulates—some particular way that things necessarily are. But if the remark really is grammatical, it does not depict any particular way that things are, even necessarily or as a matter of essence; if we really can't imagine the opposite, we can't imagine the thing itself either. Accordingly, to imply that we can is again to fall into the very emptiness we are combating.

Wittgenstein tells us that if 'Every rod has a length' is a grammatical remark, it 'means something like: we call something "the length of a rod"—but nothing "the length of a sphere" '. This does not amount to claiming that there is some specific thing we cannot imagine or conceive (namely, a sphere with a length), or that there is some specific thing that we can imagine or conceive (namely, rods with length—as opposed to what?). It amounts to noting that one expression (or range of expressions) has no use, whereas another does (which is not the same as claiming that the former range *could* not have a use; if we specify a use for them—perhaps by saying that, with respect to spheres, we call their diameter their length—then they have one). But then: in what contexts might there be any point in saying this, in noting this aspect of our use of words? The obvious one would be that of teaching the use of these words to someone who is unfamiliar with them. But a philosophical dialogue is not such a context, since the assumption there must be that one's interlocutor is as competent a speaker as oneself; and one cannot intelligibly convey grammatical information to someone who already possesses it. Can one even describe oneself as reminding a competent speaker of something it makes no obvious sense to imagine him having forgotten? If not, then how exactly is one to think of what one is doing, as a Wittgensteinian philosopher, when one directs grammatical remarks to one's interlocutor? Why should they not perfectly legitimately respond by saying 'Nonsense!' rather than by saying 'Of course!'? For in so doing, could they not rightly be thought to register a significant anxiety—not exactly that our words are meaningless (for we can easily imagine a context in which they might intelligibly say something), but rather that it is far from obvious what we might mean by saying them here and now? I shall return to this.

But for the moment I want to return to the first level of the discussion, and the proposed comparisons between two pairs of propositions. Is there more to the first comparison between the privacy of sensations and the self-sufficiency of the player of patience (otherwise known as 'solitaire') than the rest of Wittgenstein's discussion brings out? To be sure, one can imagine saying 'One plays patience by oneself' as part of an explanation of what we mean by the game of patience—picking out what distinguishes it from other games, perhaps correcting someone's misunderstanding (as evident in, say, a child asking 'Who will play patience with me?'). What would be the equivalent context for a grammatical use of the proposition 'Sensations are private'? If we have taken on board Wittgenstein's strictures in §§244 and 246, it's far harder to imagine what would betray a misunderstanding of the privacy of sensations; for their privacy is then perfectly consistent with their existence and nature being fully known and acknowledged by others, and so no one who gave expression to such points could intelligibly be corrected by pointing out that 'Sensations are private'. So would such a corrective reminder be more appropriate if issued to those who betrayed a misunderstanding of the asymmetry of knowledge and doubt in the case of sensations? This would suggest that one might usefully respond to the interlocutor of §246 ('only I can know . . . another can only surmise it') by saying 'But sensations are private!' Surely what he needs is not a reminder of that grammatical connection, but rather a reorientation of his sense of what it might mean.

This suggests that we would be better off thinking of 'Sensations are private' as part of an attempt to explain what privacy is, rather than to explain what sensations are; the point is not that this is how we use the word 'sensation', but rather that this is how we use the word 'privacy'. For if sensations are our paradigm of a private phenomenon, and yet others can perfectly well know when we have a sensation, then privacy is not best understood as a metaphysical isolation; it is better understood as the capacity to isolate myself should I choose to do so (by suppressing my expressions, or giving expression to what I am not feeling), and perhaps also as my vulnerability to others' decisions to isolate me (by not exercising their capacity to grasp what I am feeling).

This suggestion would allow us to make more sense of the comparison with 'One plays patience by oneself'; for if that comparison turned on a putative parallel between the having of a sensation and the playing of patience, then the grammatical exclusion of others from the card-game would imply a grammatical exclusion of others from one's sensation (something Wittgenstein contests with respect to knowledge in §246, and with respect to identity or ownership in §253, as we shall see). If, however, it turns on the thought that we can best understand the privacy of sensations in terms of the sense in which patience is a game for one, then the comparison would tell us that the having of sensations can as easily be played out in the public domain, and so under the eyes and responses of others, as can any game of patience. For whilst the playing of that game needs no others, it is not impenetrable to their gaze, and it does not become another game altogether when played in public. In short, sensations are private only in a sense that does not conflict with their being fully capable of public display.

One might say: the point about patience is that even patience is a game, and even games which not only can, but can only, involve one player are nonetheless followable by, and teachable to, others; the rules even of these games are inherently public phenomena, as are the moves one makes whilst playing them. In this sense, Wittgenstein means the comparison between sensations and patience to remind us that we have a language of pain, and hence that the privacy of sensations must be understood as a characteristic that may distinguish this dimension of our language from other dimensions (as patience differs from bridge), but cannot require that sensations must be essentially beyond the reach of words.

One further point of this first comparison might also be worth emphasizing. It is part of what is distinctive about patience as a game that it has (as its name suggests) an essentially passive or receptive dimension; whether the game works out is beyond the influence of individual talent and determined entirely by the disposition of cards in the shuffled pack. The player of patience is essentially subject to the ordonnance of the cards; he must suffer the fate they contain, and the same fate as would be suffered by anyone else in his place. In this sense, the centrality accorded to the player, the fact that his is the only hand in the game, hangs together with a sense of his condition as at once impersonal and out of his hands, as something given to him, something ultimately impervious to his individuality and control. If this is what the privacy of sensations is comparable with, its proper acknowledgement should involve an acknowledgement of finitude and commonness rather than a fantasy of absolute independence and singularity.

What, however, of the implied comparison between 'Sensations are private' and 'Every rod has a length'? If we take the latter together with its cousin 'This body has extension', it might seem that the point of the comparison is in fact a contrast—a contrast between grammatical remarks that serve to clarify what it means to be a material object (or a particular kind of material object—a rod as opposed to a sphere), and those that explain what it means to be a psychological (say, a mental or inner) phenomenon. If so, the force of the comparison would be to suggest that the true mark of the psychological is not immateriality but privacy—not the lack of spatio-temporal features such as extension but the fact that inner states, precisely because they have natural forms of outward expression (and so must be capable of, but need not achieve, public manifestation), are such that we can resist, misdirect, or fail to elicit another's capacity and willingness to acknowledge those expressions. In this context, to say that sensations are private is to say that they, like any other aspect of the life of the mind and heart, can be hidden.

A difficulty remains, however. For Wittgenstein attempts to illuminate the grammatical status of 'Every rod has a length' by introducing the idea of picturing what that proposition aims to say, and more specifically by claiming that the relevant picture would simply be that of a rod. Could one do the same with the claim 'Sensations are private'? What would it be like simply to picture a sensation, and thereby underwrite one's sense of the self-evidence of its privacy, the inconceivability of its being otherwise than private—which Wittgenstein tells us amounts to our having no understanding of what might be meant by picturing the opposite?

Is part of our sense of insuperable difficulty here the thought that sensations such as pain are inherently unpicturable? But if they have both learnt and unlearnt forms of public expression, why not picture a paradigmatic instance of pain behaviour—of a human body wracked by pain: say, a Grünewald *Crucifixion* or Munch's *Scream*? Would that simply be a picture of the behaviour as opposed to the pain? Would our depiction have altogether missed that which accompanies the behaviour, the important and frightful thing on account of which the man depicted cries or writhes (cf. §296)?

In §297, Wittgenstein offers a comparison:

Of course, if water boils in a pot, steam comes out of the pot and also pictured steam comes out of the pictured pot. But what if one insisted on saying that there must also be something boiling in the picture of the pot?

Cavell imagines two kinds of response to this question:

One response might be: 'Of course there is something boiling in the pictured pot! Otherwise there wouldn't be steam coming out! That there is something boiling inside is what the steam *means*! You seem not to understand what a picture *is*!' But sometimes one's response will be: 'Nonsense! How could something be boiling in a *picture*? You might as well look for something boiling in the *words* "pot with steam coming out"!' (*CR* 334)

Cavell's primary concern is to point out that both forms of response, in so far as they inherit without interrogating the suspicious insistence of Wittgenstein's imagined response to the pictured boiling pot, suffer a kind of emptiness. One insists on asserting that there is something boiling in a (pictured) pot that is for all the world boiling; the other insists that there could not be something boiling in what is for all the world a picture (of a boiling pot). The first tries to offer information to those who, in so far as they grasp what a picture is, could not conceivably be informed by it; the other insists on something that no one, in so far as they grasp what a picture is, could fail to appreciate ('A picture of a boiling pot is not itself boiling' is, one might say, a grammatical remark). Hence, neither succeeds in saying something—in meaning anything in particular by what they insist upon saying.

How might this treatment transfer to the idea of using a picture in connection with the grammatical proposition 'Sensations are private'? Might someone insist that 'That there is pain inside is what the writhing means!', and someone else that 'You might as well look for pain in the words "crucified man"!'? At the very least, to insist that any such picture either must, or could not conceivably, include the pain as well as the writhing, would suggest some misunderstanding either of pictures or of pain. For if one grasps that pictures depict, and that pain finds expression in pain behaviour, then one must grasp that a picture of a human being saying or doing something expressive of pain is both a depiction of (someone in) pain, and (because it depicts expressions of pain, hence something that might be present when pain is absent, and vice versa) a depiction of something capable of being hidden—that is, as private. In other words, to say, with respect to the Grünewald *Crucifixion*, that this (writhing) man is in pain can at best be a grammatical remark (about pain, or about pictures). Hence, in the case of pain just as much as that of the rod and its length, to imagine that sensations are private is just to picture (a person in) pain.

However, what seems most striking about Cavell's imagined responses to Wittgenstein's parable of the pot, in our present context, is that each reiterates one of the two forms of response that Wittgenstein imagines to the assertion of similarly grammatical remarks in §251 and (particularly) 252. The first imagined speaker takes the original insistent response to the boiling pot to be a matter of course, and insists upon that; the second takes it to be nonsense, and insists upon that; but 'Of course!' and 'Nonsense!' are the two modes of response to parallel remarks about rods and sensations considered in §252. The apparent moral of Wittgenstein's reflections in §§251 and 252 is that either response would, on the face of it, be equally appropriate as 'a defence against something whose form makes it look like an empirical proposition, but which is really a grammatical one' (with our inclination to opt for one over the other becoming comprehensible if we imagine how we might use pictures in connection with such grammatical remarks). If, however, Cavell is right to understand their counterparts in §297 as empty, in so far as they continue the insistence of the original response in contexts where their interlocutors cannot possibly be informed by what they insist upon, then perhaps we should also reconsider their appropriateness in §252. In particular, we should query our inclination to insist upon either—that is, to regard the privacy of sensations as the kind of thing that can be insisted upon (either as obvious or as obvious nonsense).

This idea of insistence as philosophically suspicious recurs throughout these discussions of private language; it will take centre stage in §253 (with its recollection of someone in such a discussion striking himself on the breast and saying 'But surely another person can't have THIS pain!'—to which Wittgenstein responds imperiously by saying, 'one does not define a criterion of identity by emphatic stressing of the word "this" '); and it returns us to our initial speculations, earlier in this chapter, about Wittgenstein's willingness to associate grammatical propositions with nonsense. In the present context, the moral seems to be that, when one's concern is with grammatical articulations, insistence is particularly misplaced.

First, to insist on the obviousness of anything is self-subverting, since the need for insistence contradicts the claim to self-evidence and positively invites an opposing insistence; and however empty that opposition may ultimately prove to be (whether when it insists that pictures do not boil, or when it insists that expressions of pain are not the pain itself), the insistence to which it responds must bear some of the responsibility for that emptiness. More specifically, as we saw earlier, if grammatical remarks stand in contrast with empirical claims, then they cannot convey information in the way in which empirical remarks do; so to insist upon them, quite as if things might have been otherwise, is to betray a misconception about how and why such remarks might be worth making.

In response to such insistence, one might say, as Wittgenstein says to his interlocutor in §296: 'Only whom are we informing of this? And on what occasion?' To whom, for instance, and when, might the remark that sensations are private convey information? Wittgenstein does not say that it could never do so; but he suggests that in so far as it does, it will bear on matters of meaning rather than fact. If, however, a grammatical articulation just is (as §247 has it) a way of clarifying how an expression is used, then one cannot insist that the other accept that clarification, any more than one can insist that she use that expression in the way I use it—she can, after all, use it any way she wishes, and she is (she must, logically or grammatically, be) in at least as good a position as I am to make a claim about how 'we' use it. One can only invite her to bethink herself, and see whether or not she does speak as I (say that we) do—whether or not she can accept the claim to community that is implicit in my saying to her 'that is how we use it [isn't it?]'.

To this extent, then, this methodological interlude might be thought to point towards a resolute rather than a substantial reading of Wittgenstein's work—one according to which grammatical reminders do not tap into a given, impersonal source of authority, but rather articulate a way of going on with our words that the other is invited to acknowledge but is always free to deny (if she is prepared to take responsibility for that denial—say, by finding and articulating and living by another such way). We might also think of it as discovering one way of meaning the term 'private'—that is, as acknowledging one sense in which sensations are (and could not be other than) private: viz. that they can be hidden. Since, however, this sense of privacy is entirely compatible with others knowing of one's sensations (just as the sense in which patience is a solo game is compatible with others knowing that and how one is playing it), it will not be a way of meaning the phrase 'private sensations' that will satisfy anyone who feels a compelling need for it. If anything, it suggests a certain tension within his initial characterization of what a private language is: for in so far as sensations can be said to be private in this sense, they obviously cannot be said to be knowable only by the person whose sensations they are. We remain, therefore, in search of a way of meaning what anyone attracted to that form of words really has it at heart to say with it.

5

Cavell's Corsican Brothers (§253)

IDENTITY: PAINS, COLOURS, AND CARS

If we now return from Wittgenstein's methodological interlude to the main flow of his investigation, we can see that Cavell's dispute with Malcolm (broached with respect to §246) naturally extends to encompass the latter's related reading of §253:

"Another person can't have my pains."—Which are *my* pains? What counts as a criterion of identity here? Consider what makes it possible in the case of physical objects to speak of "two exactly the same", for example, to say "This chair is not the one you saw here yesterday, but is exactly the same as it".

In so far as it makes *sense* to say that my pain is the same as his, it is also possible for us both to have the same pain. (And it would also be imaginable for two people to feel pain in the same—not just the corresponding—place. That might be the case with Siamese twins, for instance.)

I have seen a person in a discussion on this subject strike himself on the breast and say: "But surely another person can't have THIS pain!"—The answer to this is that one does not define a criterion of identity by emphatic stressing of the word 'this'. Rather, what the emphasis does is to suggest the case in which we are conversant with such a criterion of identity, but have to be reminded of it. (*PI* §253)

On the basis of the first two paragraphs of this section, Malcolm attributes to Wittgenstein the following view: the private linguist's opening assertion presupposes that pains resemble physical objects in that, with respect to both, we can make out a distinction between numerical and qualitative identity; whereas the truth is that pains rather resemble such phenomena as colours, in that no such distinction can be made out in either case. Malcolm thus reads Wittgenstein as occupying a position with respect to the identity of pains that negates or reverses that of his interlocutor; in reminding us of what it makes sense to say about the identity of chairs, he means to declare that, *pace* the interlocutor, it makes no sense to say anything similar with respect to the identity of pains. The grammar of our talk of 'pain' forbids it; it gives us a determinate answer to the question of what counts as a criterion of identity here. In this respect, Malcolm exemplifies the substantial reading of Wittgenstein.

But such a reading of §253 is certainly not compulsory. After all, the first paragraph opens with the interlocutor making a claim, and Wittgenstein simply asking how one word of that assertion is to be understood. He then asks what counts as a criterion of identity here; but rather than answering that question, he asks another. More precisely, he invites us to consider a context in which the distinction between numerical and qualitative identity can uncontroversially be drawn, and thereby implicitly invites us to ask ourselves whether the case of pain resembles this one, and if so, to what extent. Wittgenstein makes no assertion; he describes a possible object of comparison and asks us how far we would be happy to talk about pain in an analogous way.

The second paragraph of §253 underlines the openness of Wittgenstein's stance by implying that it is an open question how far it makes sense to talk of sameness of pains. Only then does he point out that, to the extent that it does make sense, it must be possible for two people to have the same pain; and he thereby implies that to the extent that it does not, there is no such possibility, and hence no possibility of meaningfully claiming, of informatively asserting, that two people do *not* have the same pain. We are free to determine which of these two ways we want to go; but neither seems to provide a reading of the interlocutor's use of the term 'my' that establishes a conception of the privacy of pain that will really satisfy him.

When Cavell accuses Malcolm of declaring an essential similarity between the grammar of pain and that of colour, and an essential dissimilarity between that of pain and that of physical objects, that are not borne out by the complex, flexible, various ways in which we ordinarily talk about these phenomena, I take him to be exploiting the unassertive openness of Wittgenstein's prose in this section, and thus to be offering one version of a resolute reading. For example, Cavell points out that, whilst it is true that colours and pains are alike in that both are counted or identified in terms of descriptions, Malcolm's claim that pains are exactly like colours in this respect requires more: it requires that pains are *only* counted or identified in such terms—that there is no sense of sameness of pain to be made out beyond 'descriptive sameness' (as there is no such sense in the case of colours). After all, we identify two cars as the same if they are both, say, 1952 MG-TDs—but even if your car and my car both satisfy that description, and so can be said to be the same (make of) car, no one would deny that there are two of them. Moreover, if two cars meet the relevant standards for being (descriptively) the same car, this does not guarantee that they are physically indistinguishable—we are prepared to tolerate a very wide physical discrepancy between the two instances (mine may be badly battered, and yours freshly hammered out and repainted, but we still have the same car). Come to think of it, something similar is true of pains: my headache might be accompanied by a twitch of my eyelid, and yours by mild nausea, but if we both meet the established diagnostic criteria for a specific kind of pain in the head, we have the same headache. So why assume that pains are self-evidently more like colours in these respects than they are like cars?

The crucial point here is not simply that Malcolm is begging the question against the sceptic, but how he is doing so. For his resistance to the sceptic is not grounded in a simple recounting of how we actually make judgements of sameness from case to case, but rather leads him to distort that ground in exactly the way he attributes to the sceptic, and for which he criticizes him. More specifically, Malcolm's use of our notion of 'descriptive sameness' detaches it from our normal purposes or interests in employing it, which (the examples Cavell cites suggest) centrally involve a concern with their cost or treatment or consequences, and not with their physical identity (which is at issue when we want to match objects in some respect or other). One might say that Malcolm fails to appreciate that, with respect to his comparisons and contrasts between pain, colour, and physical objects, the open-endness of our everyday forms of speech about them are such that he has a determination to make. Instead, he presents his determination as revealing how things must always already have been determined, and betrays Wittgenstein's purposes by simultaneously attributing just such a conception—just such a misplaced sense of necessity, a false fatedness—to him.

OWNERSHIP AND EMBODIMENT

But Cavell has more to say about Malcolm's misreading than this, and in two different dimensions. The first concerns §253's invocation of Siamese twins as an example of how two people might have pain not only in corresponding places in their bodies, but in one and the same place. Malcolm's response to this example is diametrically opposed to his response to the earlier comparison between pains and colours: he takes the Siamese twins to show that, if asked whether a pain in their common body part was one pain or two, we would have to make up or invent criteria to accommodate the case. Cavell contests Malcolm's assumption that there is a sharp line between 'ordinary' cases, where the criteria are fixed and available, and 'extraordinary' cases, where we invent them from scratch; he points out that the same conflict we feel in the case of the twins would be felt in an 'ordinary' case. If each of us has a pain, caused in the same way, in the same place on our left hand, we will be torn just as we are about the twins with a common hand; the tension lies within the ordinary, not beyond its artificially constructed borders.

Cavell further claims that the Siamese twins are not actually the right kind of case for giving the distinction between numerical and qualitative identity an application. More precisely, it will be the only kind of case we're likely to consider if we think that 'having numerically the same pain' could only have application by imagining a context in which pain is located in numerically the same place—at one and the same spatial co-ordinates rather than simply in corresponding body parts.

This is, of course, a perfectly natural line of thought, particularly if we have in mind our talk about physical objects, where difference in objective spatial location is what gives substance to our talk of numerical as opposed to qualitative (i.e. descriptive) identity; and it is further encouraged by the interlocutor's persistent Augustinian tendency to treat the question of how sensation-words are connected with sensations in complete independence of the everyday context of human interaction within which that connection is manifest. For, as we have seen, that separation encourages us to think of sensations as simply one more type of object that we label and refer to in the world—different from chairs only in that they tend to be located within other entities, namely human bodies, whose owners prove to be a handy guide to their more precise whereabouts. Whereas to be reminded of the fact that we ordinarily locate pains within human bodies—that similarity of location is a matter of their affecting corresponding parts of two people's bodies—is to be reminded that what primarily interests us about pain is that people suffer it, suffer from it, and are in need of comfort. For when the doctor enters the room in response to a frantic but insufficiently informative telephone call, she doesn't want to know how many pains there are in the room, and where they are located; she wants to know how many people in the room are in pain, and which they are.

One might say: pains are owned (and so can be disowned)—they are mine or yours or hers; they 'belong' to whoever can give them expression (thereby acknowledging them as their own, or failing to), and the kinds of response for which these expressions call or call out are themselves expressions (of particular individuals' particular forms of acknowledgement or denial of those in pain, and so of themselves). Heidegger would say that the mineness of pain reflects the fact that the human form of life is that of the being to whom mineness belongs—that creature who can either own or disown her existence, either take responsibility for her feelings, thoughts, and deeds (and so for her responses to the feelings, thoughts, and deeds of others) or fail to do so. In his view, this is why human existence is—it is part of what it means for it to be—always evaluable in terms of authenticity or inauthenticity, in terms of whether or not it gives expression to the individuality of the individual whose existence it is. The thought then arises: is the interlocutor's compulsive insistence on the uniqueness of his pains simply a misplaced attempt to defend his own uniqueness, as if to acknowledge that another might feel exactly what he is feeling ('THIS!') would amount to denying the separateness—the individuality—of his own existence?

Malcolm attempts to develop a version of this line of thought through his insistence that the distinction between numerical and qualitative identity has no application to pains. But Cavell's view is that, if we reorient our attention from the Siamese twin case, which goes too much with the Augustinian grain, we can find a use for the admittedly peculiar form of words 'numerically identical pain'.

Take a case adapted from that of the Corsican Brothers, one of whom, call him Second, suffers everything which happens to his brother, First. Whip First and Second writhes with him (not in sympathy, *seeing* what's happening; but even miles away, not knowing what is happening). Add to this the fact that Second never suffers unless First does: whip Second himself and he doesn't feel it. I assume further that there is no physical trauma produced in Second by what First undergoes. What I wish the example to create is the sense that Second feels pain because First *feels* it—so that, for example, if First is anaesthetized, Second equally feels nothing. Therefore it is crucial to the example that First be something we treat as a living body. (It is not unimaginable that it be a dummy or a doll which has some peculiar causal connection with Second. But that would not be a case of 'feeling because another feels it'.)—I think one finds that the usual philosophical remark to the effect that 'Any pain one feels will be one's own', is, though said to be logically necessary, simply false here. Second has no pain of his own; he has only First's pain. And doesn't it describe this situation to say: His pain is not just descriptively the same as First's, it is numerically the same? (*MWM* 251–2)

Malcolm's response to the advocate of privacy occludes the possibility that the numerical identity towards which he is gesturing concerns not location but ownership. What grounds the interlocutor's insistence on the privacy of his pains need not be a mistaken belief that his pain and another's pain could never have the same objective spatial location; it might be the sense that, even if two people shared one body (or had some body parts in common), they could never be said to have one and the same pain, because even pain in a common body part would have two owners. The Corsican Brothers example addresses this idea of ownership or inalienability, and hence opens up another, perhaps more plausible, interpretation of the interlocutor's motivation; but it also undermines it, because it shows that what seemed metaphysically prohibited—one person feeling another's pain—can in fact coherently be imagined. For the pain in Second's body is not, Cavell contends, Second's pain, but First's; Second is not rightly describable as feeling pain in another's body, but as feeling pains that are not his own. Second might express his pain by saying 'I am in pain', but he might equally well express it by saying 'First is in pain'; if he feels a pain in his leg, he can equally well locate it by pointing to his own or to First's leg. Which route he takes will depend on the point of expressing himself in a given context—does he want his pain to be relieved, or does he want to be comforted? Cavell's point is not that Second is in doubt where his pain is, or whose it is; what is significant is that either of each pair of ways of giving expression to his pain is equally legitimate.

However, even if we accept that this situation realizes what the interlocutor took to be indispensable if one person is ever truly to know that another is in pain, it would not in fact satisfy his (supposedly metaphysically unquenchable) thirst for knowledge of another—because it would not count as a case of knowing. Even here, neither First nor Second can rightly be said to know that the other is in pain by actually, literally, feeling his pain. It might seem that First must, when Second is in pain, know that he is; but the only pain First has is surely his own, which will—as it were—drown out Second's, leaving him no way to appreciate the individuality of what Second is feeling. First will certainly know what Second feels, and when and where he feels it—but then, so can we in ordinary circumstances; and although he will know it because his feelings tell him, which is not a route to knowledge of Second that we share, that knowledge will be too intellectual. His pain is at best the basis for an inference about Second's pain, not a mode of immediate awareness of Second's pain. The primary fact about the pain is that *he* feels it, that it is *his*.

What, then, of Second's knowledge of First's pain? Cavell is happy to say that Second not only has knowledge of First's pain, but that he *has* First's pain. The problem is that First's pain no longer contrasts with Second's; 'his pain' no longer differentiates what First feels from what Second feels, or First from Second; he is not *other* in the relevant sense. Second's knowledge is too immediate; his 'having' First's pain is an effect of that pain, not a response to it, and hence it leaves no room for Second's knowledge to count as an acknowledgement of First's expressions of pain, and hence an acknowledgement of First (indeed, Second may well know of First's pain whilst being entirely unaware of First's expressions of pain).

In other words, First and Second's relationship either accommodates the idea of knowing but resists the idea of feeling (First with respect to Second), or accommodates the idea of feeling but resists the idea of knowing, or more precisely that of acknowledgement (Second with respect to First). If, however, this imagined projection of the phrase 'numerically identical pain' cannot satisfactorily fill out the possibility that the interlocutor defines his position by rejecting—the possibility of 'knowing another's pain by feeling it'—then it cannot give that position any genuine content. For the interlocutor was only interested in the very idea of numerically identical pain in so far as he took its realization to be the only possible route for genuinely knowing another's pain; his scepticism amounted to an insistence (despairing or exhilarating, as the case may be) on the unrealizability of such knowledge. But what the Corsican Brothers show us is, first, that we can imaginatively realize a case of numerically identical pain; second, that it would not constitute a case of knowing by feeling; and hence, third, that it cannot serve to give substance to the sceptic's sense that there is something that we cannot do here—some specific cognitive achievement from which we are debarred. And in such circumstances, talk of the interlocutor's position as a kind of scepticism turns out to be empty or idling.

I pause at this point to register my uncertainty as to how far Cavell's critique of Malcolm's use of the Siamese twins example carries over to Wittgenstein's deployment of it in §253. On the one hand, Wittgenstein does not offer it as providing a context that would require us to make up criteria for counting two people's pains as numerically identical; but, on the other hand, its placement certainly suggests that he is assuming a reading of the interlocutor's interest in the criteria of identity for pains that relates his conception of the necessary distinctness of our pains to a sense of their necessary distinctness with respect to spatial location, rather than with respect to ownership.

I am also uncertain about the ease with which the Corsican Brothers case really does allow a projection of the phrase 'numerically identical pain'. This is because I would hesitate to say, without qualification, as Cavell does, that Second '*has* no pain of his own', and that 'the pain in Second's body is not Second's pain' (*MWM* 252). I can see that it makes sense to talk of the pain in Second's body as First's pain, and hence to imagine Second as saying 'First is in pain' when giving expression to what he is feeling, at least in certain contexts. But even then, he is nonetheless giving expression to what he, Second, is feeling, to *his* pains (and not just to the pains in his body), just as he is when he says 'I am in pain'—as Cavell appears to admit when he remarks that 'It is not clear whether Second *will express his pain* by saying "I am in pain" or "First is in pain"' (*MWM* 252, my emphasis). And when Second expresses pain by saying 'First is in pain', it does not follow that he is thereby giving expression to First's pain—although we might want to say that the pain to which he gives expression is both First's and his own.

The situation is thus not well expressed by saying that 'while we still have pain in two bodies, we no longer have, so to speak, two *owners* of pain' (*MWM* 252). I would be more inclined to say that, with respect to pain, Second and First remain two distinct owners of pain, each giving expression to his own, but they are not the owners of two distinct bodies—or rather, Second cannot think of First's body as straightforwardly not his own (and so, Cavell's example is not as distant from that of the Siamese twins than might at first appear). If Second writhes when First is whipped, but feels nothing when whipped himself, I would not wish to deny that Second's body remains his own (it is the body his pains are in, and also the substantial source of his active engagement with the world); but I would hesitate to say that First's body is exclusively his own (for it is where Second can locate his bodily pains, and the site of Second's sensory receptivity to the world, with all its slings and arrows). To say that when First is anaesthetized, Second equally feels nothing, does not block this line of response, but rather confirms it; for the anaesthetic (just like any other treatment of their pain) must be administered to First's nervous system, absorbed by the body that is clearly his, but not clearly not Second's.

In short, my sense of things is that the Corsican Brothers case places pressure not so much on the idea of Second being able to talk of his pains—of pains that are fully his even though they are always also fully First's—but on his being able to talk of his body—of one and only one body that is his, a singular or integral worldly existence, the single embodiment of his ability to inflict himself upon the world, and the world's ability to inflict itself on him. The body in which Second suffers is not the body that inflicts that suffering (say, by internal malfunction) or through which that suffering is inflicted (say, by injury); so Second can disown neither.

Even if my qualms here, my resistances to Cavell's imaginative projection, are justified, how much of his argument is affected? His critique of Malcolm remains, I think, essentially untouched, since my resistances to Cavell's descriptions are no more a kind of making up of criteria, an invention of new ways of talking, than are Cavell's descriptions; if we have a disagreement, it is about how to go on with our ordinary words for pains, bodies, and persons. Cavell's critique of the interlocutor might, however, be more seriously affected. To be sure, even if this imaginative attempt to show that the advocate of privacy would not want what he thinks we cannot have is a failure, it does not follow that he is giving expression to a clear or coherent desire. That remains to be settled, even perhaps by a certain re-imagining of the Corsican Brothers. Nevertheless, my resistance to his imagining of that case suggests two points of significance. First, the idea that the owner of a pain is the one who can give it expression cannot be dislodged as easily as Cavell claims; if Second can give expression to a pain, then that pain is his—even if that pain is also another's; and to the extent that we regard the interlocutor's sense that another cannot have his pains as an expression of this conviction, it remains unshaken. Second, and much more importantly, it would appear that Cavell's desire to show the interlocutor that numerically identical pain would not really satisfy the desire for knowledge that fuels his scepticism has led him to project our words in uncompelling ways, and hence to risk appearing forced or prejudicial rather than uninsistently inviting. To this extent, Cavell exemplifies a version of the same philosophical failing that he rightly attributes to Malcolm.

Perhaps, however, I am misinterpreting the intended force or point of Cavell's story about these brothers. For if I contest his interpretation of their situation, I am taking it for granted that his words are meant to present us with a conceivable, contentful situation—an imaginable human possibility; but in so doing, I may be interpreting Cavell's approach in unduly substantial (rather than appropriately resolute) terms. Perhaps the ultimate fate of that tale as Cavell tells it is rather to reveal itself to be only apparently contentful. This possibility can be seen to emerge when we recall that the earlier portions of Cavell's critique of Malcolm led him to suggest that our relations to 'other minds' are best understood not in terms of knowledge but of acknowledgement. After all, one consequence of First's hypothesized relation to Second is that we are forced to admit that First is not genuinely other to Second (his pains are too close to Second's to be acknowledgeable as his by Second); so it would seem, on reflection, to follow that this is not best understood as a case in which one person is incapable of acknowledging another person as such—as another to him, as his other. For if Cavell's sense of the centrality of the concept of acknowledgement is accurate, two people between whom a relation of genuine acknowledgement is essentially excluded cannot be thought of as two (distinct, genuinely separate) people at all; to withhold the concept of acknowledgement just is to withhold the concept of interpersonal relationship, and hence to withhold the concept of a person. One might say: the Corsican Brothers show us that to think of our pains as alienable just *is* to think away the individuality and distinctness of our existence as experiencing subjects.

On such a resolute reading of the essay, then, the final conclusion of Cavell's line of inquiry is designed to invite us to recognize that the tale of the Corsican Brothers has only the *appearance* of genuine substance. In order fully to grasp what is wrong with the sceptic's anxieties about other minds, we need not only to get to, but also to get beyond, the point from which we think we can say to her: 'I understand exactly what form you would like human relationships to have, and I can tell you that you would not have what you want even if our relationships with others did take that form.' We must ultimately come to see that there is no such point from which to address the sceptic's concerns—that there really is *nothing* genuinely substantial in the sceptic's fantasy of a position in or from which genuine knowledge of another would be possible. Hence, we cannot say to him, 'That would not be knowledge', because there is no 'that' to which to refer. One must, in other words, throw away even this rung of the ladder of words that Cavell has constructed in order to free us from our philosophical enslavement to emptiness. Accordingly, to keep standing on that rung, in order to query the propriety of its construction, amounts to failing to take the final, truly liberating step beyond our fantasies.

Even if we acknowledge the elegance and attractiveness of this reading, its acceptance will have consequences for our understanding of every aspect of Cavell's strategy. The most obvious of these involves the neatness of its fit with the actual tone and terms in which Cavell handles the Corsican Brothers, whilst always (according to this reading) aware that it presents only an illusion of sense. Take the following sentences as an example:

So here we have a pain in *this* body and a pain in *that* body, and it is numerically the same body, literally the same. The thing which looked unintelligible, was so, only given a certain picture. What has happened to make the situation intelligible is this: while we still have pain in two bodies, we no longer have, so to speak, two *owners* of pain. (*MWM* 252)

Any reader might feel that these sentences do not merely present the story as having an obvious content; they repeatedly, even bluntly, emphasize its substantiality. Is such unquestioning insistence a legitimate authorial device, even if that author feels justified in allowing or encouraging his readers to inhabit imaginatively what he will later reveal to be empty of sense? Or are matters here verging on entrapment? Or should we, rather, regard the very bluntness of Cavell's declaration of his story's intelligibility—together, perhaps, with the casual use of the potentially fateful phrase 'so to speak', at precisely the point at which he appears to tell us what this intelligible situation actually means—as implicitly inviting us to attend more closely to that aspect of his procedures?

A resolute reading of this essay also requires that we reformulate what otherwise provides a more straightforward explanation of the blunt force with which Cavell emphasizes the intelligibility of his tale; and that is what we identified as the primary function of the construction of the story at this point in the essay's dialectic. For it is presented first of all as part of a criticism of Malcolm's willingness simply to assert that the notion of numerically identical pain is nonsensical—a willingness that, in Cavell's view, shows that Malcolm is in the grip of a certain picture of pains and their identity, as well as in the grip of a certain picture of language, and indeed of the ordinary. And one might think that this multiple criticism can go through only if the tale of the Corsican Brothers is intelligible; for if it is not, then Cavell has not provided the sceptic with a way of using the idea of 'numerical identity' with respect to pains that Malcolm can be accused of excluding, through lack of imagination and an unduly rigid conception of the projectibility of words. But once again, one might argue on Cavell's behalf that the kind of imagination that he takes Malcolm to lack is not that needed to see a patently intelligible possibility, but rather a willingness to see how his interlocutor might get himself into the grip of a conviction that there is an intelligible possibility here, when ultimately there is no such thing. In other words, on the resolute reading of Cavell, he is indicting Malcolm for failing to do as much as he could and should in imaginatively inhabiting the sceptical interlocutor's perspective, a diagnostic task which essentially involves a moment of willingness to take nonsense for sense—to articulate the interlocutor's fantasy from the inside, and thus to participate in what is latently nonsensical with a view to allowing its nonsensicality to become patent.

This ought to remind us of Wittgenstein's striking association (in §§251 and 252) of grammatical reminders with nonsense; and it raises a rather more general question about this aspect of what I am calling resolute strategies with respect to philosophical nonsense. For if the final resting-place of Cavell's emancipatory dialectic is a conviction of the sheer emptiness of the sceptic's imaginings, then proponents of the substantial strategy such as Malcolm are likely to point out that they reached the very same terminus in rather shorter order. What, then, is to be gained by taking a much longer route to that conclusion—and doing so in a way which involves aiding and abetting the reader in taking nonsense for sense? Is the thought that we could not properly have grasped the internal relation of personhood and otherness or acknowledgement except by going through this attempt to give content to the sceptic's fantasy? This will not seem plausible on the face of it to the substantial reader; for why should such grammatical connections be capable of elucidation solely through their more or less elaborate misuse, as opposed to a careful attention to their role in our lives? Or is it, rather, that when fantasy or the illusion of sense (as opposed to falsehood or distortion) is our target, the ways in which fantasies inhabit and inform our thinking, and so our lives, are such that they can be dealt with decisively only by exploding them from within?

This, it seems to me, is where one might begin to see a genuine distinction between resolute and substantial approaches to philo-sophical nonsense, and discern reasons for choosing the former. For if one's interlocutor is convinced that her empty words articu-late an insight, then simply to oppose or dismiss them (by directly invoking a grammatical articulation that they appear to violate) would fail to acknowledge the fact that she will necessarily respond to that invocation from within her conviction—for example, by feeling that her point must have been misunderstood, or that she has discovered something that undermines her, and our, prior investment in that article of grammar. Such direct confrontation would also fail to acknowledge the fact that a speaker no less competent than oneself has been able honestly to get herself into the grip of such a fantasy. It would, in short, amount to failing to take one's interlocutor seriously—failing to acknowledge her as a fellow-speaker, as one's other; and it is not hard to see the self-subverting irony, as well as the sheer hopelessness, in this way of attempting to recover (for her, and for ourselves) the grammatical significance of the concept of acknowledgement for our concept of a person.

SPEAKING FOR THE SCEPTIC

This sketch of a case for the resolute reading is implicit in the further dimension to Cavell's critique of Malcolm to which I adverted earlier. For it is central to Cavell's understanding of ordinary language philosophizing that appeals to what we say when we cannot directly repudiate any sceptic about other minds. Simply pointing out that the sceptic's words do not cohere with what we ordinarily say cannot constitute a satisfying response to him (because any serious sceptic will account for it); it provides no grounds for believing the sceptic's use to be nonsensical (since it is of the nature of words that they be sufficiently flexible to be projectible in various ways into new contexts), and it is grounded solely on the philosopher's competence as a speaker, a competence that can be claimed equally legitimately by the sceptic; hence it stakes a claim that can have authority over the sceptic only if he freely acknowledges that it does so.

This means, first, that the ordinary language philosopher is at the mercy of his opponent, in that a test of the pertinence of his criticism must be whether those to whom it is directed accept its truth; he is thus obliged imaginatively to inhabit the sceptic's perspective, in part because he won't elicit the sceptic's admission that his convictions have been properly dealt with unless he gives them accurate expression, and in part because he is not properly acknowledging whatever gives the philosopher himself any authority if he does not seriously attempt to imagine how anyone might find himself driven to say what the sceptic says. As Cavell puts it: 'In all cases, the problem is to discover the specific plight of mind and circumstances within which a human being gives voice to his condition. Scepticism may not be sanity, but it cannot be harder to make sense of than insanity, nor perhaps easier, nor perhaps less revealing' (*MWM*, 240–1).

On Cavell's view, Malcolm's response to the sceptic makes no attempt to discover his plight of mind and circumstances. Malcolm writes as if the sceptic simply cannot be serious, can have discovered nothing which his words are trying, perhaps in more or less forced ways, to convey, but has simply (for no obvious reason) begun to misuse his words, whilst refusing (for no obvious reason) to see or do anything about that 'fact'. Malcolm fails to see the sceptic's words as ones that might seriously be meant by another human being, and thereby fails properly to acknowledge the sceptic as another, equally competent speaker, another speaking out of the common human condition. In short, he fails properly to acknowledge the sceptic as other to himself, whilst claiming to inherit an approach to philosophy that is inherently committed to the methodological internalization of such acknowledgement.

When Cavell himself tries to imagine the plight of mind and circumstance for which scepticism about other minds is an apt expression, he finds himself invoking some very specific feelings and experiences. He articulates a feeling of powerlessness with respect to others that is not an inability to do anything in particular;

he presents himself, in sceptical mood, as 'filled with this feeling—of our separateness, let us say—and I want you to have it too. So I give voice to it. And then my powerlessness presents itself as ignorance—a metaphysical finitude as an intellectual lack' (*MWM* 263).

What interests me here is not the way in which an apprehension of finitude finds expression in a claim of ignorance, but the nature of the underlying apprehension. A feeling of powerlessness with respect to others that is not an inability to do anything in particular is like a feeling of dependence that is not a dependence upon anything in particular, or a feeling of safety that is not safety with respect to any particular danger; both are ways of using words that resemble the kinds of use that Wittgenstein elsewhere refers to as employments of terms in a secondary sense.

This analogy may seem to limp if we have in mind as examples of secondary senses of words the question of whether Wednesday is fat or lean, or that of the colours of vowels; the sharing of a sense that such questions even make sense, let alone the sharing of a sense of how they should be answered, may seem too fragile and idiosyncratic a matter to have a bearing on Cavell's attempted expressions of scepticism. But it is worth noting that Wittgenstein's discussion moves from Wednesday's girth to coloured vowels via the example of the relation between calculating and calculating in the head—a secondary use of words that is not obviously fragile or idiosyncratic (cf. *PI* p. 216). And anyway, the point of the analogy here is the underlying relation between primary and secondary senses that all three examples are meant to illustrate—one in which the primary sense does not license the secondary sense, but the secondary sense is incomprehensible unless one grasps the primary sense, and the use of the very same word even in this very different context is felt to be indispensable.

Such a relation certainly seems to be exemplified in the present context. The notion of powerlessness has its primary use in contexts where one is powerless to do something specific, and yet we use that same word in a context where there isn't anything particular that we cannot do as the only apt expression of our feeling; and the comprehensibility of our expressions therefore depends on whether those we address can follow such turnings of our common words beyond their familiar language-games—on whether they can find their feet with us here, find that their own experience of life with others has included vicissitudes that they might naturally articulate in such terms, or find instead that they have lost their footing with us altogether.

If a capacity of this kind is what underlies a proper apprehension of what is given distorted expression in scepticism, then any adequate ordinary language response to the advocate of privacy must have three interrelated aspects. It must find room for the concept of acknowledgement in any grammatical investigation of what it is to know another person; it must ensure that its responses to those who question or deny the possibility of such ack(knowledge)ment themselves properly acknowledge their competence as speakers and their common humanity; and it must be capable of acknowledging the kinds of feelings and experiences that will find proper expression, if they find it at all, only through secondary uses of words.

In the penultimate paragraph of his essay, Cavell offers the following remarks:

A natural fact underlying the philosophical problem of privacy is that the individual will take *certain* among his experiences to represent his *own* mind—certain particular sins or shames or surprises of joy—and then take his mind (his self) to be unknown so far as *those* experiences are unknown. (This is an inveterate tendency in adolescence, and in other troubles. But it is inherent at any time.) There is a natural problem of *making* such experiences known, not merely because behaviour as a whole may seem irrelevant (or too dumb, or gross) at such times, but because one hasn't forms of words at one's command to release those feelings, and hasn't anyone else whose interest in helping to find the words one trusts. (Someone would have to *have* those feelings to know what I feel.) Here is a source of our gratitude to poetry. And this sense of unknownness is a competitor of the sense of childish fear as an explanation for our idea, and need, of God... At least we can say that in the case of some mental phenomena, when you have twisted or covered your expressions far or long enough, or haven't yet found the words which give the phenomenon expression, I may know better than you how it is with you. I may respond even to the fact of your separateness from me (not to mention mine from you) more immediately than you. (*MWM* 253)

This is not simply a reminder of one way in which anyone might come to a sense of their unknownness, and hence to verge upon a sense of unknowability; it is also a portrait of the straits in which the sceptical advocate of privacy finds himself, and a portrait of Cavell himself. In order to think of himself as such, the sceptic takes a certain experience (of powerlessness, of separateness) to be representative of who he is; when he finds this experience uncomprehendingly dismissed, he feels himself to be denied, unacknowledged; and he can only find acknowledgement through a philosopher prepared to take an interest in his experience, to recognize the degree to which it is twisted or covered over by the forms of words the sceptic commands, and to provide acceptable words for its proper expression. Such a philosopher would be responding to the fact of the sceptic's separateness more immediately than the sceptic himself; and he would thereby earn the kind of gratitude that some bestow on the poet, others on the psychoanalyst, and still others on God.

But in order so to acknowledge the sceptic, this philosopher must give voice to scepticism—must present himself to his readers as having had the feelings to which the sceptic gives distorted expression. This means that, in denying the sceptic's unknownness, he risks unknownness himself—not just the denial of the particular experiences he shares with the sceptic, but the denial of himself as a philosopher in so far as he gives those experiences expression in his philosophizing. In short, his existence as a philosopher is staked on the hope that, even with experiences so penetrating and personal that their proper release demands that one trust oneself to secondary uses of words, others will find themselves able to acknowledge those words as expressions of their own individual responsiveness to the world. In this kind of philosophy, words inevitably risk becoming private currency, unable to convey anything intelligible to another; and hence the idea of a private language—the fantasy or threat it represents—will appear to penetrate to the heart of the philosopher's sense of himself.

6

Wittgenstein's Semi-Colon:
Second Methodological
Interlude (§255)

The philosopher treats a question; like an illness. (*PI* §255, my translation)

In a recent review of a collection of Karl Kraus's aphorisms, Michael Wood tells us that Erich Heller has called the punctuation in this remark the most profound semi-colon in literature.[1] Without going quite that far—without even knowing exactly how far one would be going, and in which direction, in accepting Heller's judgement—one must acknowledge that Anscombe's translation of this remark ('The philosopher's treatment of a question is like the treatment of an illness') fails to do justice to the concision and multivalence of the German original; more precisely, it conflates one way of interpreting the original with the original itself. To be sure, Wittgenstein's German allows for (even, perhaps, encourages us to settle for) the possibility that the philosopher treats a question as one treats an illness; but it also allows for the possibility that what is like an illness is not the question but the philosopher's treatment of

---

[1] In the *London Review of Books*, 24/5 (7 March, 2002).

it, and even for the possibility that it is the very inclination to talk or conceive of philosophers as treating questions that is like an illness.

These other possibilities might be easier to envisage if we bear in mind that *behandelt* invokes not solely the idea of (medical or psychoanalytic) courses of treatment, but also ideas of dealing or trading with—hence the idea of doing or cutting a deal with—and ultimately of course the idea of handling (say, guiding, soothing, even manipulating) something. And if this emphasis on that single term seems unbalanced, it is worth bearing in mind that Wittgenstein prepares the ground for his aphorism in the preceding section precisely by italicizing this word, and placing it at the climax of his train of thought:

The substitution of 'identical' for 'the same' (for instance) is another typical expedient in philosophy. As if we were talking about shades of meaning and all that were in question were to find words to hit on the correct nuance. That is in question in philosophy only where we have to give a psychologically exact account of the temptation to use a particular kind of expression. What 'we are tempted to say' in such a case is, of course, not philosophy; but it is its raw material. Thus, for example, what a mathematician is inclined to say about the objectivity and reality of mathematical facts, is not a philosophy of mathematics, but something for philosophical *treatment*. (*PI* §254)

The irony of re-presenting the conclusion that fine shades of meaning have nothing to do with philosophy proper in the form of an aphorism, and one which activates the fine shades of meaning implicit in the key term of that conclusion, is hard to deny (although easy to miss). More specifically, one might ask: if what a mathematician is inclined to say about the nature of mathematical phenomena is not philosophy, but its raw material, what is the status of what a philosopher is inclined to say about the nature of philosophy? Is that, too, simply raw material, standing in need of philosophical treatment; if so, treatment of what kind? And which way of expressing this philosopher's inclination is to be subject to such treatment—that essayed in §254, or that essayed in §255? Or is it rather that the unvarnished—indeed, the brusque, dismissive, even condescending—line of thought in §254 about the irrelevance of fine shades of meaning to philosophy is the raw material here, and its aphoristic reformulation in §255 an instance of what its proper philosophical treatment might or should look like? If so, then the latent moral of this sequence must be something like the reverse of its apparent one; for in §255, fine shades of meaning are all, and the philosophical value of the thought will be internally related to its literary form—will depend on the extent to which it finds words which hit on the correct nuance.

Which brings us back to our original question: how are we to understand the various possibilities of sense held open by the placing of that semi-colon in §255? The first, most obvious possibility depends upon comparing a philosophical question to an illness or disease: but translating *Krankheit* as 'illness' rather than 'disease' holds open a further set of possibilities within this one, in so far as it underlines the fact that the kind of treatment we envisage being required in the philosophical case will be determined by whether we compare the philosopher's question to a medical problem (one affecting, let us say, the body) or to a problem of the mind or soul—the domain of psychoanalysis (not to mention religion). If we prefer the medical interpretation, we will think of philosopher's questions as essentially diseased or abnormal: they can have no intrinsic value or interest, but rather require extirpation—a kind of philosophical surgery—in order to re-establish health. And then it will seem obvious that, whilst medical intervention is preferable to non-intervention once the philosopher's question has taken root, the best of all possible worlds would be one in which the question never puts down those roots (perhaps a global immunization strategy is required). In short, the medical interpretation of ideas of illness and treatment leads us quickly to the conclusion that philosophy itself is essentially diseased—a pathology of human culture, something that purely and simply damages the realm of the ordinary.

If one interprets the same idea psychoanalytically, this set of conclusions remains open, but is no longer forced upon us. For whilst there *are* understandings of psychoanalysis which treat it as a process for restoring mental health, for readjusting the psychologically abnormal so that they might fit more smoothly into the self-evidently valuable routines of everyday social interaction, it can be understood otherwise. It can, for example, lead to conclusions about the individual, spiritual costs of struggling to fit into a routinized everyday realm; about the contingency, hence fragility and variability, of our ideas and realizations of mental normality or well-being; about the extent to which ordinary adulthood is not only constructed out of, but is also inherently pervaded by, impulses, drives, and fantasies that resist control, sublimation, and repression.

This kind of psychoanalytic model of philosophical questions would, if anything, suggest the mutual imbrication of philosophy and the everyday, not their simple opposition; and its model for their therapeutic treatment would correspondingly put in question the authority otherwise invested in the analyst over the patient (in large part because of the authority invested in certain notions of what is pathological and what is not, hence of what is normal or healthy and what is not). For the Freudian picture of the relation between analyst and patient involves not only transference but counter-transference: the drives and impulses at work in the patient, and so in his understanding of his analyst, are just as much at work in the analyst's understanding of his patient and their relationship (and so in his understanding of himself). And Freud famously, if not consistently, claimed that an analytic treatment could be deemed to have reached closure (however provisional) only with the patient's acknowledgement of the correctness of the analyst's interpretations.

If we stay with this picture of philosophy as therapy, then the second of the three possibilities of sense to be found in §255—the possible comparison between illness and the philosopher's *treatment* of the question (rather than the question itself)—begins to emerge; for then certain ways of claiming or assuming authority on the part of the philosophical therapist will seem to be further expressions of the very difficulties that the therapist claims to be treating (with a view to removing). In other words, the way in which one handles philosophical questions, and hence questioners, can either be consistently informed by the broader understanding of those questions on which one claims to be basing one's treatment, or it can contradict it—and in such a way as to manifest precisely the confusions supposedly being addressed. As we have seen, this is a constant theme of Cavell's treatment of Malcolm's supposedly therapeutic treatment of those drawn to the idea of a private language; Cavell's sometimes rather rough handling of Malcolm aims at revealing that Malcolm's extremely rough handling of this philosophical question is simply one more manifestation of the scepticism it claims to diagnose.

What, however, of the third possibility—the possibility that the very idea of the philosopher as treating a question is itself comparable to a disease or illness? To some extent, this simply brings out a further implication of the second possibility: if certain interpretations of the idea of treatment are continuous with the disease under treatment, then the same must be true of any conceptions of a philosopher's relation to his questions which embody such interpretations. But one might also consider the possibility that Wittgenstein is equally concerned to diagnose other implications of this general model of treatment.

To begin with, any talk of philosophers treating their questions implies a certain kind of distance between the philosopher and the question, and a certain kind of activity on the part of the philosopher: the question comes to him from without, and he deals with, handles, manipulates—anyway, exercises some control over—it. This closes off the possibility that he might equally well find himself in the grip of such questions, hence actually asking them rather than primarily having them addressed to him, or anyway articulated in his hearing, and so might find himself under treatment. And in a related way, it closes off the possibility—even the necessity—of a moment of receptivity in his relation to the question; it might be an essential part of his work as therapist to simply submit to the question, to allow himself to be handled or treated by it. This might mean allowing himself to acknowledge that some of his own inclinations or confusions find expression in that question; but it might also mean allowing the question to put his own initial ideas of how to respond to it—of what it signifies and, more specifically, his sense that it may well signify nothing whatever—in question.

One might think of this as the philosophical equivalent of counter-transference—the philosopher's willingness to subject his own unavoidably active orienting sense of the meaning (or the obvious nonsensicality) of these questions to treatment. After all, if one of philosophy's central tasks is to put in question what other disciplines take for granted in their work, the philosopher cannot consistently refuse to do the same with even the most fundamental of his own guiding methodological assumptions. Hence, the philosopher's tendency to assume or to say certain things about philosophy, even (perhaps especially) the inclination to compare philosophy to therapeutic treatment, must itself be open to philosophical treatment.

The point here—a point underlined not only by Wittgenstein's aphoristic re-presentation of his methodological remarks, but also by his use of the semi-colon as the pivot of his aphorism—is not to choose between these three possibilities of sense (or between the various sub-possibilities within each), but to note that all are in play, and that they should be in play. For genuinely philosophical questioning must not only respond to questions directed towards it, but must maintain a questioning stance towards its responses, and so towards its characterizations of what it is doing in so doing. By allowing us to link the idea of an illness with every key term in the clause preceding its semi-colon, this aphorism keeps the sense and weight of every element of Wittgenstein's self-conception open to question.

First, the fact and the form of §255 question the picture that §254 presents of philosophy's relation to fine shades of meaning, and hence to language, and hence to its own forms of expression. Second, by focusing our attention on the philosopher's treatment of *questions*, it invites us to attend to the fact that the second and third sentences of §254 utilize the idea of what is and is not questionable in philosophy's relation to words in a manner which suggests that this matter is not itself a fit topic for questioning—as if it is beyond question what is or is not in question when we do philosophy. In this way, §255 also gives us distance or perspective not only on the apparent content of that preceding line of thought, but also on its tone—with its apparent and substantial disdain for those more resolutely inclined philosophers for whom nuances of meanings matter, to whom they might be a means of conveying genuine information or insight (as the word *Auskunftsmittel*, which Anscombe translates as 'expedient', might more literally and less prejudicially be translated). For that disdainful tone, with its assumption of a therapeutic authority that is both unearned and in conflict with a persistent register of this therapeutic author's own work, stands as much in need of philosophical treatment as the thought it informs. After all, who, more than any other competent speaker, has the authority to say whether and when a nuance of meaning is of no real philosophical significance? And who, whatever their competence with words, could treat this question a priori—in advance of its emergence in the context of a particular philosophical question?

One might say: in philosophy, being tone-deaf is like an illness.

7

Wittgenstein's Diarist: Three Readings (§258)

Let us imagine the following case. I want to keep a diary about the recurrence of a certain sensation. To this end I associate it with the sign "S" and write this sign in a calendar for every day on which I have the sensation.— —I will remark first of all that a definition of the sign cannot be formulated.—But still I can give myself a kind of ostensive definition.—How? Can I point to the sensation? Not in the ordinary sense. But I speak, or write the sign down, and at the same time I concentrate my attention on the sensation—and so, as it were, point to it inwardly.—But what is this ceremony for? for that is all it seems to be! A definition surely serves to establish the meaning of a sign.—Well, that is done precisely by the concentrating of my attention; for in this way I impress on myself the connexion between the sign and the sensation.—But "I impress it on myself" can only mean: this process brings it about that I remember the connexion *right* in the future. But in the present case I have no criterion of correctness. One would like to say: whatever is going to seem right to me is right. And that only means that here we can't talk about 'right'. (*PI* §258)

For those attracted to a substantial reading of Wittgenstein, the logic of this passage is clear.[1] The question is: can the diarist

---

[1] For an exemplary instance of such readings, see my *On Being in the World: Wittgenstein and Heidegger on Seeing Aspects* (London: Routledge, 1990), Ch. 3.

establish a meaning for his term 'S'? If so, it must be possible to define that meaning, for the grammar of meaning is such that a coherent practice of employing a word presupposes a standard of correctness for its use. The diarist attempts to establish this by impressing on himself the connection between the sign and the original sensation; future candidate sensations will correctly be called 'S'-type sensations if they resemble the original sample sensation, otherwise not. Since, however, the original sensation may not endure, it can function as a standard of correctness in this way only if he can remember it accurately. But, as Wittgenstein points out, to be able to remember the original sensation correctly, we must be able, in principle, to distinguish memories of 'S' from memories of other sensations (call them 'T' and 'U'); but we could only do so if we already had a standard of correctness for the use of 'S' (since talk of a 'memory of S' can be meaningful only if 'S' is meaningful). But this process of using our memory is supposed to be the means by which we establish that standard of correctness; unless it is successfully completeable, no such standard is available. In effect, in order to remember what 'S' means, the diarist must be able to remember the sample of 'S'; but in order to be in a position to do that, he must know what 'S' means. Hence, what the diarist calls 'private ostensive definition' does not merit the term 'definition'; and 'S' accordingly does not merit the appellation 'meaningful term'—not even when its meaning is supposed to be accessible only to the diarist.

For those attracted to a resolute reading of Wittgenstein, the preceding account is subtly but decisively misleading. For the true significance of §258 is given in the sections which frame it:

. . . But what does it mean to say that [someone] has "named his pain"?— How has he done this naming of pain?! And whatever he did, what was its purpose?—When one says "He gave a name to his sensation" one forgets that a great deal of stage-setting in the language is presupposed if the mere act of naming is to make sense. And when we speak of someone's having given a name to pain, what is presupposed is the existence of the grammar of the word "pain"; it shows the post where the new word is stationed. (*PI* §257)

... Then did the man who made the entry in the calendar—make a note of *nothing whatever?*—Don't consider it a matter of course that a person is making a note of something when he makes a mark—say in a calendar. For a note has a function, and this "S" so far has none. (*PI* §260)

The concept of pain has a very particular place in our lives. Pains are given expression in what we do and say; what is said about the pain by the person who has it is given a position that is different from what others say about that pain; we draw distinctions within the general category of pains between mental suffering and physical suffering, and many more distinctions within both subcategories—distinctions that come out in the ways we treat or seek or avoid them, the ways we value certain kinds of poetry and literature and life projects, and so on.

We can imagine people whose concept of pain, whilst akin to ours, is also importantly different from it. We might, for example, (following Cora Diamond) consider a variation on the case of the tribe that Wittgenstein mentions in *Zettel*, §380.[2] They take pity on those with visible injuries, but not those with no visible injury; they use a different term for such cases, and people who complain are mocked. They do not defer to the reports of the injured person in either kind of case; our question 'Where does it hurt?' is treated by them as we treat the question 'Where is it bleeding?' A suffering tribe member may be able to say that his elbow hurts without looking, but if there is no visible injury he is treated as we treat those lacking the normal proprioceptive capacity to say where one's limbs are without looking.

Mindful of this example, we might ask: Does the diarist's concept of pain resemble our own concept of pain, or that of Wittgenstein's

[2] Cora Diamond, 'Rules: Looking in the Right Place', in D. Z. Phillips (ed.), *Wittgenstein: Attention to Particulars* (London: Macmillan, 1989), 12–34; Wittgenstein, *Zettel*, 2nd edn. (Oxford: Blackwell, 1981).

tribe? Or is it akin to ours, but different in a different way from that of the tribe? Or is it akin to another kind of sensation, and if so which? Is his use of 'S' a rule-governed activity at all, or just a behavioural regularity, or an irregular nervous tic? What gives us so much as the idea that what he is doing is using a sign, when all there is to his 'use of "S" ' is that he sometimes makes a noise or makes a mark? Each hypothesis I have invoked has as much and as little to be said for it as any other; which means that none has anything to be said for it. We have not yet given any substance to the idea that what we are confronted with is the use of a word, let alone a specific kind of use of a name for a specific kind of sensation.

But we must not assume that this amounts to giving a negative answer to the following question: Recording our pains in a diary is something we do in the ordinary circumstances of our lives; could we do so in very different circumstances—for example, when our note making does not hang together with any other behavioural expressions of our sensations? For that way of putting things suggests that there is, on the one hand, a practice of recording pains, and on the other, the broader circumstances of our lives, in which that practice has a particular place; and the issue is whether that practice could survive if the circumstances changed. According to the resolute reading, for us to engage in that kind of activity just *is* for us to behave in ways that have this kind of place in our lives, these kinds of connection with a vast range of other things we say and do. Hence, §258 does not show us that something (noting the occurrence of our pains) is logically impossible in the kind of context the diarist stipulates; it shows us that, although we thought that we were imagining someone noting the occurrence of his sensations, we were not imagining anything—any specific human activity—at all. The issue is not whether impressing on oneself a connection between sign and sensation is enough to make that sign the name of that sensation; Wittgenstein's aim is to get us to see that 'the tale of the diarist' amounts only to someone making a mark, or uttering an inarticulate sound.

What reason have we for calling "S" the sign for a *sensation*? For "sensation" is a word of our common language, not of one intelligible to me alone. So the use of this word stands in need of a justification which everybody understands.—And it would not help either to say that it need not be a *sensation*; that when he writes "S", he has *something*—and that is all that can be said. "Has" and "something" also belong to our common language.—So in the end when one is doing philosophy one gets to the point where one would like just to emit an inarticulate sound.—But such a sound is an expression only as it occurs in a particular language-game, which should now be described. (*PI* §261)

One might wonder whether the form of the above set of sentences is in tension with its apparently resolute content; for it makes its philosophical point (about the extent to which even the most minimal characterization of a term carries its distinctive weight only within the context of a particular form of life with words) in a way which makes it seem that the conditions of genuine speech constitute a kind of penal limitation—as if the claim that noises have meanings only in the context of a language-game were an adamantine necessity imposed upon our natural inclinations from without, and now reimposed in Wittgenstein's voice upon our natural philosophical inclinations. Can such remarks really just be reminders of what we could not fail to know? If so, then their tone draws upon memory's capacity to afflict us, to inflict something upon us, to recall us to something painful.

We need to recall here that the idea of emitting an inarticulate sound has appeared earlier in the discussion, in §244's invocation of a primal scene of teaching a child words for his pain. In that context, the child's cry is inarticulate, but hardly inexpressive, or somehow prior to genuine human expression—it is filled with his pain, to which his elders respond (even if austerely). It is as if Wittgenstein's way of expressing himself here, in response to one in the grip of a conviction that the idea of a private language has meaning, is deliberately intended to align his relation with his philosophical interlocutor with that between the child and his elders. I suggested earlier that the tale of the crying child pictures the advent of language and society as traumatic—as something to be suffered, and as always already taking on an aspect of self-harm—as if the achievement of articulacy (the capacity to achieve a perspective on oneself, hence the capacity for selfhood) involved the loss of an impossible but seemingly paradisal self-sufficiency.

Seen in this context, the interlocutor's imagined inarticulate sound is not merely noise: it is expressive of pain, of an essentially twofold trauma. First, it registers his pained awareness of 'bumps that the understanding has got by running its head up against the limits of language' (PI §119); more precisely, it indicates a trauma consequent upon the traumatic accession of language as such—our apparently unshakeable sense of its limits as limitations or restrictions that engender frustration and suffering, rather than as conditions to be suffered or accepted. Wittgenstein's more penal turns of phrase and tone, those moments when his grammatical reminders seem to lay down the law, invite us to contemplate this aspect of our relation to our (linguistic) finitude, and acknowledge that his philosophical method cannot but seem like a re-infliction of this punishment, a reiterated 'Thou shalt not'. And the only way of overcoming this sense of affliction depends upon a second traumatic moment: that attendant upon the internalization of a philosophical vocabulary—of 'language-games' and 'forms of life', of meaning taken in relation to use—and so of a particular mode of attending and responding to the world of one's experience, a particular kind of self-possession. For with that internalization goes an inevitable sense of dispossession: the loss of a certain impossible ideal of philosophical self-coincidence and self-assurance, of the self's transparency to itself in philosophy, beyond any allegiance to the common round of human life, and the everyday words that thread through it.

Cavell's reading of §258, in *The Claim of Reason*, is not best understood as a version of the resolute rather than the substantial approach; it is in fact deeply, and fascinatingly, orthogonal to that dispute. For he reads its opening not as an attempt to give substance to an imaginative flight (which both the substantial and the resolute readings aim to reveal as empty, even if in different ways), but rather as describing an everyday banality. Cavell imagines Wittgenstein's unusually long pause after these sentences as acknowledging that there is nothing wrong with this so far; such diary entries might have a very specialized use, but 'there might be lots of reasons for wanting to keep track of this sensation, medical or psychological or spiritual reasons' (CR 345). Hence, the diarist's difficulties in forging a connection between sign and sensation do not constitute an argument against a possible (or an impossible) deed; but neither are they essentially marginal to the business of seeing the emptiness of the idea of a private language. These difficulties are real, but they are of the interlocutor's making.

Notice that Wittgenstein's claim that "here we can't talk about 'right'" reaches back only three or four sentences, just to the idea of "impressing the connection on myself", ie getting the sign and the sensation stamped upon one another, so that, so to speak, their faces can be seen to match quite independently of any decision of mine. (I undertook to do everything by myself necessary for providing something with meaning; then I spend untold energies trying to convince myself that I have done it.) If there were no need for the idea of "impressing" the connection, then the objection about nothing or everything counting as "right" would have no force. . . What creates the sense of needing, or wanting, the special impressing? (CR 348)

The moment Wittgenstein makes a remark about the definability of the sign, despite the fact that what he indicates is true *ex hypothesi* about any sign in a genuinely private language, the diarist responds with an anxious insistence that he is able to define it to himself, by private ostension or association. And when the reliability of that association is queried, he responds by anxiously invoking a picture of impressing the connection on himself. The core verb here—*pragen*—conjures up stamping an image on a coin, as the Queen's head is stamped on British coins to declare that they are at once legal tender and the property of the Crown. But the diarist's assumption that such embossing of his experiences upon his signs is necessary, when for all the world he has clearly explained how he uses the signs to record his experiences, suggests that he doesn't straightforwardly believe his own story. As Cavell puts it:

In each of Wittgenstein's attempts to realize the fantasy of a private language, a moment arises in which, to get on with the fantasy, the idea, or fact, of the *expressiveness* of voicing or writing down my experiences has to be overcome. In section 243 this is quite explicit; in section 258 the idea of formulating a definition of the sign overcomes the fact that the sign already has all the definition it needs—if, that is, I am actually employing it as I said I was. (CR 348)

What anxieties might obliterate the expressiveness of our actions in making a note in our diary, leading us insistently to offer incoherent procedures for enforcing a connection that Wittgenstein has not so far denied is there? Cavell sees two central possibilities. The first is that we fear that our expressions do not in fact signify anything—that our best, our simplest and most straightforward, attempts to give utterance to how things are with us, utterly fail to do so; so our insistence on enforcing connections between signs and sensations directly expresses our lack of belief in their existence. The second possibility is that we regard our natural capacity to give expression to how things are with us as threatening betrayal and exposure—as threatening our privacy; so we insist on the need to enforce connections between our signs and our sensations, and create the impression that no procedure can properly fulfil it, in order to distract ourselves (and others) from their real existence.

So the fantasy of a private language, underlying the wish to deny the publicness of language, turns out, so far, to be a fantasy, or fear, either of inexpressiveness, one in which I am not merely unknown, but in which I am powerless to make myself known; or one in which what I express is beyond my control. (CR 351)

As a reading of §258 on its own, this interpretation is immensely powerful; in particular, it motivates the unusually long pause preceding Wittgenstein's first response to the diarist, and it brings out its real peculiarity. For it is unclear how someone who emphasizes throughout his philosophizing that one can only make a remark if there is a point to doing so, could allow himself to remark on the indefinability of the diarist's sign, when that feature of it is obvious to all. But if we read it as an uninsistent way of raising a question, however faint and dismissible, about the security of the sign's connection with what it records, in order to see just how quickly and excessively the diarist will react to it, and thereby to uncover the anxieties that possess him, then its philosophical point becomes rather more clear.

If, however, we recall the immediate textual context of §258, it seems harder to maintain the plausibility of Cavell's presentation of the diarist's efforts as just one example of the everyday ways in which we give voice to our experiences. For the burden of §§256 and 257 is to fill out the idea of a private language when its words, unlike our own, are not tied up with our natural expressions of sensations. In §256, the idea of associating signs with sensations is explicitly presented as one that the private linguist must construct for himself, in the absence of any natural pain behaviour; and §257 emphasizes that he cannot then simply take for granted the stage setting of our ordinary life with language that shows us what 'naming sensations' really amounts to. This makes it hard to read the opening sentences of §258 in Cavell's way, since the impression he creates of the diarist having to repress the expressiveness of his entries depends upon our imagining him doing so in the ordinary circumstances of life, equipped with a grasp of the grammatical post where the new sign is to be stationed.

Even if my hesitations about Cavell's decontextualization of §258 are well-founded, however, there are other dimensions of his reading that we have thus far overlooked, and that merit attention. They emerge if one looks more closely at Cavell's reading of Wittgenstein's initial response to the diarist; for although he sees Wittgenstein as accepting the diarist's practice as everyday, he also sees him as registering a sense of the peculiarity—more precisely, the highly specialized function—of the sign he has constructed.

The entry 'S'... was simply and solely to be inscribed by me on just those occasions on which something happened to me. Is this itself why Wittgenstein remarks that there is no definition of it?—as if to say: The sign's sheer *being* there is all that matters; its use is all the meaning it has, and in this case the use never varies. Something similar could be said about the ordinary asterisk as well, used as a superscript to indicate a footnote. But while its use never varies, there may be other marks also consigned to this identical use; and the asterisk must still be distinguished from this. It is the merest convenience that there should be marks of this kind at all; the same purposes could be accomplished by special spacings between words, or elevations of them. (If all of written language were devoted to such purposes—if all of it were as it were not really part of language but part of the convenient machinery of writing—then could there be dictionaries? The case would seem to be that all of this dictionary would look like specialized parts of dictionaries now look. And I think one can say that a complete dictionary of such a language would have to contain tables that include *everything that could be said* in the language, as if everything sayable took the form of an idiom.) (*CR* §347)

Here, Cavell elucidates another aspect of the verb *pragen*, on which so much of §258 later pivots; for the word invokes, beyond embossing or stamping coins, the idea of coining new terms—for example, neologisms—and thereby other specialized linguistic purposes—for example, idioms. Taken as invariant writing mechanisms, such coinings plainly threaten the idea that the diarist's procedures might be a way of founding a language—for what would words be like if they were never projected into new contexts?—and thereby associate this moment in Cavell's writing with the resolute strategy's concern to elucidate an element of fantasy latent in the interlocutor's position. But Cavell quickly moves in a different direction, as he fills in a realistic context for such notational procedures:

One can imagine a writer for whom it becomes of interest to note a dozen different states of mind in which he or she writes; we might imagine the margins of his or her manuscripts lined with asterisks, ampersands, checks, sharps, loops of various eccentricity, each noting the occurrence of one or more of these states. Certain writers might feel that it was essential to the significance of what they were writing that these experiences be incorporated (not necessarily stated) in the body of their text, as part of the course of their prose. Wittgenstein is such a writer. (*CR* §348)

Cavell earlier imagined the diarist's signs dissolving into the spaces between, or into an elevation of, the broader prose that makes up his diary—as if its attenuated use is such that it need not be a separate, self-sufficient mark. Here, he imagines its use by a writer for whom it must not be a distinct, marginal annotation—its burden must rather find unassertoric, uninsistent but pervasive expression in the main body of his or her text. Cavell names Wittgenstein as such a writer, and hence implies that Wittgenstein can be read as responding positively to the diarist's story because he sees an internal relation between himself and his interlocutor, sees himself in the other's fantasy or fear of a certain kind of expressive prose style. But since Cavell's own identification with Wittgenstein in this respect is hardly a secret; and if we recall Cavell's prefatory description of this part of his own text as 'the keeping of a limited philosophical journal', whose reading by others would be pointless or hopeless 'until the life, or place, of which it was the journal, was successfully, if temporarily, left behind, used up' (*CR* p. xxiii); then it is hard to avoid concluding that Cavell too is, and means us to understand him to be, but without his stating that he is, a writer of this kind—and hence that he too sees himself in the diarist's fears or fantasies.

This speculation receives a certain kind of confirmation in a parenthetical passage embedded in a broader consideration of the diarist's compulsion to insist on connections between sensations and signs that exist without any such insistence.

I may dedicate a lifetime to the effort to convey the meaning a small budget of words has for me. I may be one of a circle of people so dedicated, even to the same words. I would hardly have come to this verge, supposing I am of sound mind, if I thought that *no* one else *could* understand my words. But suppose I came to think this. Then either I would doubt that I myself attached real meaning to them, and I would make ready to leave the circle; or else the least of my problems would concern my definition of a word—I mean my formulating it or pointing out its meaning. My problem has become one, let us say, of bearing the meaning. Nothing of me but is impressed with the word. (*CR* 349)

Suppose that this small budget of words is embodied in a text called the *Philosophical Investigations*, and that the circle comprises those concerned to inherit Wittgenstein, understood as a writer to whom it is essential that the life or place of which his words are the expression be incorporated in the body of his text. Then Cavell's glancing reference to the threat of insanity not only invokes the ideas evident in his earlier essay on these issues (with its emphasis upon the ordinary language philosopher's obligation to give voice to those experiences of the sceptic that are both representative of his existence and utterly dependent for their effect upon his interlocutor's acknowledgement of their penetration to his most private and fragile responses to the world). It also implies that the experience of reading texts which harbour such a philosophical ideal will itself be subject to the same fears and fantasies—a fear of all but inevitable inexpressiveness, a fantasy of all but impossible community, and a sense that there is nothing of oneself that is not given expression, and put at stake, in Wittgenstein's words, and hence in the burden of bearing their meaning even when one comes to feel that no one else could understand what they mean—either to Wittgenstein, or to this reader of Wittgenstein, the one who is at once still within the circle and aiming to inscribe a new circle outside it, through acts of reading so personal as to form the possibility of communication without the support of convention, but with the hope of their becoming the source of new conventions.

8

Excursus: Cavell's Mezuzah

Since this image of a circle carries the stamp of another American philosopher, with whom the circle of readers of Cavell might be familiar, I'd like—before moving on—to link it to another such image, invoked when Cavell links the question of the usefulness of the diarist's signs for another with that of a certain religious practice: 'The sign in question just is one for which there is no reason to think you *have* a use (as you have no use for my name tapes, or no use for a mezuzah)' (*CR* 348). In earlier essays,[1] Cavell has much to say about Emerson's allusion to a mezuzah, when in 'Self-Reliance' he declares: 'I shun father and mother and wife and brother when my genius calls me. I would write on the lintels of the door-post, *Whim*. I hope it is somewhat better than whim at last, but we cannot spend the day in explanation.' And what is it, for Emerson, for one's genius to call? 'To believe your own thought, to believe that what is true for you in your private heart, is true for all men—that is genius. Speak your latent conviction and it shall be the universal sense; for always the inmost becomes the outmost.' Cavell glosses this as follows: 'Something which is of the least importance, which has no importance whatever but for

---

[1] Here I cite 'Thinking of Emerson', and 'An Emerson Mood', both collected in *The Senses of Walden: Expanded Edition* (San Francisco: North Point Press, 1981), hereafter *SW*.

the fact that it is mine, that it has occurred to me, becomes by that fact alone of the last importance; it constitutes my fate; it is a matter of my life and death. If we could know in advance of departure after whim that it will truly prove to have been our genius that has called us, then the gate to salvation would not be strait; there would be little need for faith, and little to write about' (*SW* 154–5).

But what of what whim, or genius, so understood, would have you do? Cavell says this:

Literal writing on the door-posts of one's house is more directly a description of the mezuzah (a small piece of parchment inscribed with two passages from Deuteronomy and marked with a name of God, which may be carried as an amulet but which is more commonly seen slanted on the door frame of a dwelling as a sign that a Jewish family resides within). (The spiritual danger in putting Whim in place of the name of God will seem a small thing to one convinced that the name of God is mostly taken in the place of whim.) Accordingly, we should consider that the writing contained in the mezuzah explains why the mezuzah is there, why God has commanded that it be there. (*SW* 155)

Why, then, is Cavell's mezuzah there, in the body of this discussion of privacy? Perhaps because the fantasies and fears of the diarist with which Cavell identifies impress on him (and drive him to impress on us) a connection between the diarist's notation of his whims and certain writers' ways of marking the name, or the place, or the life of God, and hence of the self in relation to God. More precisely, he associates the most intimate and penetrating forms of self-realization with both religious and anti-religious inflections of the idea of self-overcoming or self-dispossession—a willingness to divest oneself of what seems most vital to one's continued existence, in the name of that continued existence.

The wish underlying the fantasy [of necessary inexpressiveness] covers a wish that underlies scepticism, a wish for the connection between my claims of knowledge and the objects upon which the claims are to fall to occur without my intervention, apart from my agreements. As the wish stands it is unappeasable. In the case of my knowing myself, such self-defeat would be doubly exquisite: I must disappear in order that the search for myself be successful.

These words may express a significant truth. They form a homonym of the truth, a kind of sentence-length pun, a metaphysical irony. If so, this serves to explain why writing on the part of those who have some acquaintance with the topic of self-knowledge—Thoreau or Kierkegaard or Nietzsche, for example—takes the form it does, of obsessive and antic paradox and pun, above all of maddening irony. As if to write towards self-knowledge is to war with words, to battle for the very weapons with which you fight. (*CR* 351–2)

So when Cavell, in his private diary, says 'Nothing of me but is impressed with the word', which word, in his small budget of words, might this be? If it cannot but be 'whim', must it not also, always, be a displacement of a name of God? And can such a displacement ever be so twisted or wrenching as entirely to lose touch with that which it displaces?

9

Wittgenstein's Gift (Of Grammatical Imagination): Pots and Dolls, Stones and Flies (§§ 268–9)

Why can't my right hand give my left hand money?—My right hand can put it into my left hand. My right hand can write a deed of gift and my left hand a receipt.—But the further practical consequences would not be those of a gift. When the left hand has taken the money from the right, etc., we shall ask: "Well, and what of it?" And the same could be asked if a person had given himself a private definition of a word; I mean, if he has said the word to himself and at the same time has directed his attention to a sensation.

Let us remember that there are certain criteria in a man's behaviour for the fact that he does not understand a word: that it means nothing to him, that he can do nothing with it. And criteria for his 'thinking he understands', attaching some meaning to the word, but not the right one. And, lastly, criteria for his understanding the word right. In the second case one might speak of a subjective understanding. And sounds which no one else understands but which I *'appear to understand'* might be called a 'private language'. (*PI* §§268–9)

By conjoining the idea of a private definition of 'pain' with that of the right hand giving the left hand a gift, Wittgenstein recalls the idea first introduced in his tale of the crying child in §244—that the ability to articulate one's inner life is something suffered or given from without (by others), and hence amounts to the internalization of otherness. If the term 'private definition' really meant what it is intended to mean, then language as such would be the mere appearance of a gift; more precisely, it would fail to amount to the genuine internalization of otherness, for it would abolish the necessary distance or difference between giver and receiver, and thus abolish any real internalization of that difference. It would therefore ensure that the further practical consequences of the acquisition of language would not include that of genuine selfhood.

§262 puts the matter the other way around:

It might be said: if you have given yourself a private definition of a word, then you must inwardly *undertake* to use the word in such-and-such a way. And how do you undertake that? Is it to be assumed that you invent the technique of using the word; or that you found it ready-made? (*PI* §262)

Of course, one point of this remark is to emphasize that meaning is a matter of patterns of use, ways of going on with words; another is to hint at the paradoxicality of trying to found language on the interior performance of a speech-act—one of the techniques of the language the would-be definer has supposedly not yet acquired. But the pivotal question, 'how do you undertake that?', might further be read as stressing the difficulty involved in giving undertakings to oneself—as, for example, an explicit commitment or promise to give oneself money. Cavell articulates the difficulty as follows: 'Can't I trust myself and make a promise to myself? But I cannot hold myself to my promise to myself, perhaps because I am in no position to refuse my excuses' (*CR* 391). The practical consequences of writing out deeds of gift and receipts to oneself are not those of a gift—any more than calling to mind how a timetable looked has the practical consequence of a justification of my original memory of the train's time (*PI* §265), or laying my hand on top of my head has the practical consequence of a measurement of my height (*PI* §279).

Again and again, the believer in a private language is forced to treat the putative speaker of such a language as if he were always already divided or double, capable of being both measurer and measured, justifier and justified, giver and receiver: it is quite as if two people inhabit this body, each with its own hand (and the face a battleground between them—cp. *PI*, §286). He thereby implicitly acknowledges the internal relation between the acquisition of language and the acquisition of selfhood; but his depiction of it amounts to a painful parody—as if enacting a regression to the self-enclosed, even self-harming behaviour of Wittgenstein's child in §244—because it fails to acknowledge that both forms of articulation presuppose a relation to that which lies outside or beyond the self, since both presuppose an internalization of genuine otherness.

Nietzsche once defined the human being as the animal who makes promises, the promising animal; and Wittgenstein's tale of the gift might be seen as exploiting the same ambiguity in the related idea of undertakings or commitments. For promising is not just one way in which saying is doing, a paradigm of speaking as the taking on of commitments, for which one is then responsible in ways that can outrun our best intentions and foresight; promising oneself money might more specifically seem to promise an enhancement or appreciation of one's capital, one's resources for the future—a mode of self-enrichment made possible by earning (that is, at once meriting and deriving) a kind of interest in and from oneself. If one could fulfil such a promise, it would allow us to fulfil our promise, to realize or achieve more of what we could be—to become who we are, as Nietzsche would say; and such self-overcoming implicitly embodies an idea of the self's differentiation from itself, its irreducibility to what it presently is, maintaining its openness to the future in so far as it maintains an interest in that aspect of itself that is unattained but attainable. The would-be private linguist thinks that the promise of such self-realization might be fulfilled entirely autonomously or solipsistically, by granting oneself initiation into words; Wittgenstein aims to put that picture of self-reliance in question, but only in order to replace it with a better one—one which accepts the link between language and selfhood as self-differentiation, but rejects the possibility of their self-origination. For his tale suggests that to be in a position genuinely to give my word, and so to think of words as mine to give (which means thinking of myself as a genuine self, capable of taking responsibility for my words and deeds, owning rather than disowning them—hence as giving myself in and through giving my word), I must first receive them, take them from others.

Such a reading of §268 might suggest that, for Wittgenstein, the very idea of private definition short-circuits or breaks down in just the way his idea of self-giving or self-promising self-destructs, and hence that the idea of a private language founded on such definitions must be similarly self-defeating—simply null and void. But §269 does not seem to fit this reading at all; indeed, its final sentence appears to establish a use for the phrase 'private language', and one with which Wittgenstein himself seems comfortable—quite as if he means to crown our attempts to give meaning to that phrase with success.

To be sure, Wittgenstein is in fact determining a use of the phrase 'private language' that aims to underline rather than subvert the point that that same phrase has no apparent meaning in the mouths of those who claim to believe in such things. In other words, he is saying that, in such people's discourse, the phrase 'private language' is simply part of what he (Wittgenstein) means by a private language—that is, a sound that those philosophers who employ it merely seem to understand even though in reality neither they nor anyone else does. The rhetorical structure here is thus ironic or humorous, rather than straightforwardly self-subverting.

But then the question inevitably arises: why not simply claim that the phrase in question has no meaning, or that the private linguist fails to mean what he wants to mean by it? Why take it up into one's own discourse, and find a way of meaning it—even if that way might serve to highlight the private linguist's failure to mean anything by it? Indeed, one might further ask whether Wittgenstein *has* succeeded in finding a coherent way of meaning it. He certainly seems to supply or at least imply criteria for applying the expression under scrutiny; but is our sense that we understand its use anything more than mere appearance?

How might I appear to understand sounds which no one else understands? If we accept the implications of the preceding sentences of §269, those sounds must appear to mean something to me alone; I alone must appear to be able to do something with them. Adverting to §268, I might begin by uttering the sound quietly to myself, with the familiar blank gaze of introspection, as if preoccupied with my own inner state, and then go on to put that sound to use—perhaps with the occasional appearance of self-correction, but mostly with an untroubled resort to its utterance in a variety of contexts, such as a diary. (We might think of this as a pared-down analogue of the person in §237, who produces an incomprehensibly irregular wavy line from an utterly straight original with a pair of compasses.) But of course, I must seem to understand those sounds in a particular way *even when no one else can*. This means imagining a situation in which the criteria for understanding are, for all the world, satisfied in my case, and yet the usual concomitants and consequences are absent—no one else satisfies the criteria for merely thinking they understand, let alone those for understanding correctly; no explanations or disagreements or communication of any kind are possible with respect to these sounds, and so on.

It is vital to recall that, although we may have only an appearance of understanding, understanding is nonetheless precisely what it is an appearance of. It would be as wrong to claim that use of the term 'understanding' is simply ungrounded here as it would be wrong to claim that it is straightforwardly grounded; and the same holds true of the linked terms 'definition' and 'language'. Is this not, after all, a further lesson of Wittgenstein's tale of the right hand trying and failing to give the left hand money? On the one hand, the practical consequences would not be those of a gift; on the other, the patterns of exchange (of deeds, receipts, and money) between the two do precisely mimic those of a genuine exchange of gifts. The only sense we can make of what we see—that is, seeing it as a mere appearance or semblance of gift giving—depends upon seeing the link between what these hands are doing and what two people exchanging a gift actually do.

There is a parallel here between Wittgenstein's tale of the gift, and his sequence of interrelated tales (in §§265–7) about justifying claims concerning timetables, clocks, and bridges. The basic moral of these tales is stated as follows:

Looking up a table in the imagination is no more looking up a table than the imagined result of an imagined experiment is the result of an experiment. (*PI* §265)

In like manner, one might say, determining what time it is by looking at a clock in the imagination is no more a way of determining what time it is than imagining a justification of the choice of dimensions for a bridge is a way of justifying that choice. But in all three cases, it is legitimate to talk of what we are doing in our imagination—that is, to talk about what we are imagining—as precisely looking up a table, looking at a clock and, for example, making a loading test. It makes sense to talk of what we are imagining in such terms; and the sense it makes is dependent on the connection between what we are imagining and what counts as actually doing whatever it is that we are imagining doing. As in the case of the gift, words are migrating from a public context, in which their significance is a matter of the way they hang together with various concomitants and consequences, into a more private or personal or subjective one, where it is the individual's inclination to reach for those words despite the absence of their normal context that grounds our ability to determine what they are doing—that is, exactly what it is that they are imagining.

One might say that, in order for anyone to fulfil our criteria for imagining something, they must always already have exercised their imagination—they must have seen, and seen the point of, a certain extension of their ways with words; more precisely, they must have accepted a certain way of internalizing or introjecting them, must have gone on to articulate their inner life in terms first made available to them by their public life with words and with all the things to which words apply. But the point here is not just that, without that imaginative capacity, they would not have the kind of inner life whose reality and nature are at stake in these discussions about privacy. It is equally to the point that, without it, they would not be in a position to conflate actual and imaginary modes of justification in the ways that engender the fantasy of a private language; and further, that, without it, they would not be in a position to overcome those fantasies in the ways favoured by Wittgenstein himself. For if we go back over the key stages of his discussion of these fantasies, we see the would-be private linguist repeatedly inclined to displace words from their familiar public context into a personal one which lacks their familiar accompaniments (as with 'undertaking', 'giving', 'justifying', 'measuring'); and we also see Wittgenstein responding to the expression of these weird inclinations by appealing to the very capacity that is presently under critical examination.

Any list of such instances would include: 'Let us imagine a table . . . that exists only in our imagination' (*PI* §265); 'Let us imagine the following case' (*PI* §258); 'it would also be imaginable for two people to feel pain in the same . . . place' (*PI* §253)—not to mention such related injunctions as 'Here is one possibility' (*PI* §244); 'But suppose I didn't have any natural expression for the sensation' (*PI* §256); 'Well, let's assume the child is a genius and itself invents a name for the sensation!' (*PI* §257). The reflexive or doubled invocation of the imagination at the beginning of §265 is particularly striking: it amounts to asking us to apply our imaginative capacity to the domain of the imagination itself, and in this respect it recalls the complex methodological discussion of §251, where the claim that my images are private immediately engenders the response that one can't imagine the opposite, which in turn generates an inquiry into what such defensive invocations of the imagination might mean when grammatical rather than empirical limits are at issue.

The present context provides us with a further perspective on this conjunction of the imagination and the domain of grammar, by reformulating the question of how far the imagination is essential to our capacity to determine articulations of grammar. For, on the one hand, Wittgenstein is emphasizing a qualitative distinction between genuine or actual justifications and merely imagined or imaginary ones; on the other, he does so by inviting us to exercise our imaginations with respect to the applicability of the term 'justification'. But if his claim is correct, how can it be justified? If the relevant distinction is brought out primarily or essentially by means of the imagination, how can that count as its receiving a genuine justification rather than the mere appearance or semblance of one? We can rightly say that grammar guides our imaginations, or finds expression in the limits and inflections of what we find imaginable; but then we must also say that our imaginations determine grammar—that the limits of sense are given by our ability or willingness to find a context inviting or discouraging the projection of a given word. If so, is Wittgenstein's philosophy somehow necessarily beholden to the very capacity it criticizes, and so bound to distinguish between authentic and inauthentic ways of exercising the imagination in philosophy?

Furthermore, if we are capable of finding ways of meaning and understanding words that take them out of or beyond their more familiar public contexts—as with 'understanding', 'definition', 'language', 'gift', and so on—then in what sense can we have faith in the existence of grammatical limits beyond which we—and certainly the would-be private linguist—must not or cannot go? Here, it might help to go beyond our present textual context, and invoke the discussion provoked by Wittgenstein's claim (in §281) that 'only of a living human being and what resembles (behaves like) a living human being can one say: it has sensations; it sees; is blind; hears; is deaf; is conscious or unconscious'.

"But in a fairy tale the pot too can see and hear!" (Certainly; but it *can* also talk.)

"But the fairy tale only invents what is not the case: it does not talk *nonsense*."—It is not as simple as that. Is it false or nonsensical to say that a pot talks? Have we a clear picture of the circumstances in which we should say of a pot that it talked? (Even a nonsense-poem is not nonsense in the same way as the babbling of a child.)

We do indeed say of an inanimate thing that it is in pain: when playing with dolls for example. But this use of the concept of pain is a secondary one. Imagine a case in which people ascribed pain *only* to inanimate things; pitied *only* dolls! (When children play at trains their game is connected with their knowledge of trains. It would nevertheless be possible for the children of a tribe unacquainted with trains to learn this game from others, and to play it without knowing that it was copied from anything. One might say that the game did not make the same *sense* to them as to us.) (*PI* §282)

Can we imagine a case in which people ascribed pain only to dolls? It would have to be one in which only a highly attenuated version of our criteria for pain (and our criteria for responding to those in pain) would have application, and in which the point of such applications would float free from its normal links to the use of such terms in the context of animate beings. But the analogous case of children playing trains (unlike other instances of secondary sense cited later in the book, such as 'calculating in the head'—*PI* p. 216) suggests that we could not, or at least should not, altogether reject the possibility of such an exercise of the imagination. What we should rather do is acknowledge that, if it were possible, it would have consequences: for the point or sense, the meaning, of the self-originating game would differ from its derivative counterpart as much as that of the two games of trains differs for the two tribes of children. Moreover, even if the would-be private linguist's uses of words can be said to have a point only in so far as we view them as parasitic upon the familiar public uses of words in ways they mean to deny, this means that they may have a kind of sense or significance to which we would do well to devote some attention—if, for example, we mean to understand their motivation or purposes in so displacing words.

Wittgenstein pushes our imaginations one step further:

Look at a stone and imagine it having sensations.—One says to oneself: How could one so much as get the idea of ascribing a *sensation* to a *thing*? One might as well ascribe it to a number!—And now look at a wriggling fly and at once these difficulties vanish and pain seems able to get a foothold here, where before everything was, so to speak, too smooth for it. (*PI* §284)

The dialectical and figurative complexity of this passage repays some consideration. After issuing an order to our imaginations, Wittgenstein then ventures to imagine for us how we might respond to it—specifically by imagining that we have discovered a categorical mismatch between thinghood and feeling, call it objectivity and subjectivity. Then he reveals that mismatch to be itself merely apparent, by ordering us to look at a wriggling fly. (Is he imagining that we will actually look around for such a fly, or rather that we will simply imagine one? Would contemplating an imaginary fly actually have the effects he is about to specify?) The idea of pain's application in the context of *this* (animate) kind of thinghood is conveyed by the figure or image of its gaining a foothold on an apparently smooth surface; and this image, which first invites us to imagine the fly's movements replacing the smooth surface and unruffleable calm of the stone, further incites us (or is this just my imagination?) to imagine the wriggling fly actually alighting on the stone, and showing by its fidgeting that the stone's apparently smooth surface is in fact sufficiently rough-textured for its feet to find a grip.

This says more than that the field of thinghood or objectivity should not be envisaged as monolithic or singular, but rather as finer-textured or more various, at least to the extent of discriminating animate from inanimate things. It further invites us to imagine what we might say if someone invited us to imagine viewing stones themselves, or at least some kinds of stones, as capable of inviting the application of such terms as pain—if, perhaps, we look not at a smooth pebble but at a larger, heavily abraded flint with a deep cleft in its side. The novelist and philosopher Iris Murdoch has imagined characters who are perfectly capable of such thoughts; here is one of them, a young woman named Moy, thinking to herself:

The whole world was a jumble of mysterious destinies. Did the stones who were picked up by human beings and taken into their houses *mind*, did they dislike being inside a house, dry, gathering dust, missing the open air, the rain, perhaps the company of other stones? Why should she think that they must feel privileged because she had, out of a myriad others, discovered them and picked them up? She felt this weird anxiety sometimes as she caressed a rounded sea-worn pebble or peered into the glittering interior of a flint.[1]

Do we understand what Moy is thinking or feeling here? Is her anxiety weird, and hence comprehensible as such; or is it—and the passage of the novel which depicts it—nonsense? Is this a clear picture of the circumstances in which we should say of a young woman that she thinks that stones have sensations? It is not obviously akin to a nonsense-poem, or a child's inarticulate babbling (another recurrence or harking back to the crying child of §244?)—although it may be thought of as an articulate expression of a young woman's adolescent sufferings (or of her mode of suffering adolescence). Perhaps, as the novel's titular invocation of

---

[1] Iris Murdoch, *The Green Knight* (London: Chatto & Windus, 1993), 109.

an Arthurian legend suggests, it is most akin to a fairy-tale—about which I am inclined to respond to Wittgenstein's opening question in §282 in the manner that I am inclined to imagine he wants us all to respond: by saying that it is neither false nor nonsense. After all, we can all do something with and in response to fairy-tales, and nonsense-poems, and babbling children—even if it is not exactly what we do with the same words in other contexts (which is not to say that it is entirely unrelated to those doings); we know how to tell or recite or join in with each of them, and how to go on with them—some of us even know how to create them.

Even if one nevertheless wanted to say that the idea or the words of this fictional woman or that fairy-tale pot *were* nonsense, at the very least Wittgenstein is warning us to consider the variety of things that one might mean by saying that. For on his taxonomy, not all nonsense is devoid of sense, or meaning, or point; each variant of the species may in fact manifest significance in its own distinctive way. One might think of our earlier discussion of the would-be private linguist's idea of private definition as a kind of self-giving or self-undertaking as Wittgenstein's way of illuminating the significance of that particular piece of nonsense—for example, the significance of the fact that it persists in picturing the internal structure of the self on the model of relations with others, whilst repressing the fact that the former is an effect of (and not simply a precondition for) the latter. And one might also think of his earlier willingness to contemplate the thought that grammatical remarks are a kind of nonsense (in §252)—but a kind whose significance resides in the therapeutic goals of the philosophical context in which they are made.

Of course, I do not mean to overlook the fact that, in §283, Wittgenstein simply asserts that 'I do not transfer my idea [that living things can feel] to stones, plants, etc.'; but I do wish to emphasize that what he asserts is not simple. For he speaks here in the first person, not the third person, and what he speaks of is a fact—no less, but no more. He is not, in other words, articulating a universal grammatical prohibition; he is noting that the basis or ground of his, and to some yet-to-be-determined extent our, investigation is an aspect of our (cultivated) natural responses or inclinations. And in so doing, he brings into focus the fact that, and the variety of ways in which, we all transfer our words (and the ideas they articulate—such as pain, or gifts, or clocks, or tables) from one context to others, or fail to. Our willingness to do so is not further justified (say, by appeals to pre-given grammatical rules), which is not to say that we implement it without right (*PI* §289); and it is subject to cultivation or seduction—in large part because it is interwoven with our capacity to imagine or re-imagine the world of our experience in ways that invite the application of words where previously we could see no foothold for them.

Accordingly, it would never be advisable to say that nothing could count as a private language, or a private definition, or an undertaking or promise or gift to oneself; the question is whether, in making out any given way in which phenomena might so count, we have satisfied the desires or the imaginations of those (including ourselves) who have been inclined to invoke them as self-evidently meaningful.

10

The Human Manometer (§270)

Let us now imagine a use for the entry of the sign "S" in my diary. I discover that whenever I have a particular sensation a manometer shews that my blood-pressure rises. So I shall be able to say that my blood-pressure is rising without using any apparatus. This is a useful result. And now it seems quite indifferent whether I have recognized the sensation *right* or not. Let us suppose I regularly identify it wrong, it does not matter in the least. And that alone shews that the hypothesis that I make a mistake was mere show. (We as it were turned a knob which looked as if it could be used to turn on some part of the machine; but it was a mere ornament, not connected with the mechanism at all.)

And what is our reason for calling "S" the name of a sensation here? Perhaps the kind of way this sign is employed in this language-game.—And why a "particular sensation", that is, the same one every time? Well, aren't we supposing that we write "S" every time? (*PI* §270)

On the face of it, the moral of this exercise of the philosophical imagination is to utilize a manifestly public and hence intersubjectively comprehensible use of 'S' as the name of a sensation to establish that there is no logical space in any such context for the possibility of misrecognition of one's sensations. But even if one is inclined to agree with that conclusion for reasons that Wittgenstein has identified in earlier remarks, it is hard to see how this imaginary tale gives it any further support.

For why should the discovery that a particular sensation (whose presence we choose to express or note by using the sign 'S') is correlated with a rise in blood pressure give us any additional reason to think that the supposition of a mistake in identifying the sensation itself was mere show? Anyone who thinks that misrecognition of sensations is possible will hardly be convinced to change her mind simply by drawing her attention to the possibility of a correlation of that kind; she will rather take it that the threat of misrecognizing the sensation will in fact undermine the usefulness of the correlation. Of course, misrecognition *would* be an irrelevance if we took it that the pertinent correlation is actually between my being inclined to enter 'S' in my diary and my blood pressure rising. This is a view that Wittgenstein's text encourages precisely by claiming that regular misidentification of the actual sensation would not matter; for if I *could* tell that my blood pressure is rising despite misidentifying the sensation, that could only be on the basis of my *thinking* (often wrongly) that I am having that sensation. But to say that misrecognition would be an irrelevance for that reason would amount to saying that the actual presence or absence of a sensation would be an irrelevance—for the usefulness of our utterances of 'S' would then no longer be dependent on their being responsive to or expressive of my actually having a particular sensation. In short, if 'S' really is the name of a sensation, Wittgenstein's conclusion about misrecognition simply begs the question against his opponent; and if it is not, his conclusion is valid but irrelevant to its purported subject-matter.

One might say: the invocation of the manometer looked like a functioning part of the mechanism of an argument, but in fact it is a mere ornament; so Wittgenstein's apparently central claim that the supposition of misrecognition is purely ornamental in relation to the mechanism of our language-games with sensations cannot engage with our reason (our mental machinery) on that basis.

Two things follow. First, in so far as we unquestioningly invoke Wittgenstein's imaginary tale as an authoritative basis upon which to accuse his interlocutor of failing properly to distinguish between mere ornament and genuine functionality in our everyday ways with sensation-words, we thereby implicate ourselves in a version of the very same error (with respect to §270's way with sensation-words). The terms of our criticism indict us; in our eagerness to identify motes of confusion in others' eyes, we miss the beam in our own. And second, an essential part of our error lies in failing properly to categorize Wittgenstein's concluding parenthetical image with respect to the very distinction it embodies. For it should not be seen as itself a mere ornament, a purely decorative figure unrelated to the functioning heart of his investigation. Rather, its content and location, and hence its belated, uninsistent, but retrospectively obvious invitation to reconsider our initial categorization of the elements of the preceding paragraph (and hence our own relation to that paragraph) in the terms it articulates, are an essential component of the textual mechanism for sequentially arousing self-confidence, self-subversion, and self-criticism in his readers—call it the educative engendering of impersonal shame—that manifests Wittgenstein's complex philosophical designs on them.

But this textual mechanism is more extensive and more complex than we have so far discovered; and those further complexities emerge when we bring the second paragraph of §270 into our considerations, and allow its pair of questions to be heard as genuine rather than simply rhetorical. For what exactly *is* our reason for calling 'S' the name of a sensation? The moment we take this question seriously, we realize that there is a certain ambiguity in the answer Wittgenstein provides: 'Perhaps the kind of way this sign is employed in this language-game.' For is that 'way' meant to refer *solely* to the fact that we employ it as an indicator of a rise in our blood pressure (which is, after all, the elaborately overt business of the first paragraph—its way of imagining a use for entering the sign in my diary)? If so, it manifestly provides no good reason in itself for regarding 'S' as the name of a sensation: for the rise in blood pressure to which it refers is not a psychological phenomenon but a physiological one. If, on the other hand, we think of 'the way we employ "S"' as referring to our use of it as the name of a particular sensation that we discover is correlated with a rise in blood pressure, then we can certainly imagine also using it as an indicator of rising blood pressure; but its function as a sensation-name would not then be established by the business with the manometer, but would rather be presupposed by it.

In fact, a careful reading of the first paragraph of §270 shows that that is exactly how Wittgenstein's imaginary tale seems to treat its central sign. Despite beginning by invoking the diarist in §258, who precisely fails to establish a use of 'S' by inwardly associating it with a particular sensation, in the first sentences of that paragraph Wittgenstein simply takes it for granted that he can directly apprehend the relevant sensation, and so can use 'S' as a means of recording its presence. Nothing about the discovered correlation between that sensation and rises in blood pressure is presented as giving us any reason to think of 'S' as naming that particular sensation; rather, it is only if we assume that it can and does successfully refer to that sensation that its being entered into my diary can serve the additional function of indicating a rise in blood pressure. In other words, the very thing that gave the diarist most difficulty in §258—the forging of a connection between a sign and a sensation—is effected offstage with no apparent difficulty in §270; what instead occupies centre stage, and has preoccupied so much existing commentary on the section as a whole, is rather the possibility of turning an essentially psychological utterance to essentially physiological purposes. It is as if the manometer is part of a magician's performance—the heart of his elaborate, apparently central rituals of power that in fact function as distractions, directing our attention away from the first, really efficacious move of the conjuring trick (cp. *PI* §308).

In this respect, one might say that Cavell's undeniably questionable claim about the diarist in §258 is manifestly true of the diarist in §270. For here, Wittgenstein uninsistently takes for granted our everyday powers of self-expression, but his interlocutors—and his readers—find it all too easy to pass over or repress that fact about his text (and hence themselves), and instead devote themselves to more or less patently unsuccessful attempts to invent or secure that expressive capacity in some other way. But in §270, that 'other way' involves matters of physiology. So the question arises: why would Wittgenstein devote his imaginary tale to this rather specialized and essentially supplementary or parasitic possibility, and thereby tempt his readers to assume that its particular lineaments were somehow the heart of the psychological matter? That is just the reason (cf. *PI* §39).

In succumbing to Wittgenstein's proffered temptation, we first of all reveal ourselves to be constitutionally inclined to conflate the psychological with the physiological, the inwardness of the mind with the inwardness of the body. In one sense, of course, rising blood pressure *is* an inner phenomenon—but that just means that it is a physical event occurring inside the body, as opposed to other species of physical events that are immediately manifest on or occur clearly beyond the surface of a body (in the world of which that body, or rather the person whose body it is, forms a part). But this is not the sense in which sensations are inner phenomena—the sense in which they pertain to a person's thoughts, feelings, and attitudes, as opposed to occurrences in their bodies. Nevertheless, we compulsively conflate linguistic indications of mental as opposed to bodily life with linguistic indications of activities occurring under the skin as opposed to beyond it; we picture human skin as if it were the interface between mind and body rather than between body and world.

Such literalizing interpretations of our entirely legitimate talk of the inwardness of our thoughts and feelings suggest a deep tendency on our part to depict the reality of our inner life in terms of the integrity of our bodies—as if violations of privacy were physically penetrative acts, and revelations of that privacy were a kind of self-flaying, literally turning ourselves inside out. Is this what Wittgenstein means by his later references to the way in which philosophy is full of (misunderstood or mishandled) illustrated turns of speech, or full-blown pictorial representations of our grammar (*PI* §295)? If so, it suggests that our implicit awareness of the internal relation between mind and body is subjected to an impoverished or reductive conception of what that might amount to. It is to such doggedly literal modes of thinking that Wittgenstein's famous aphorism—'The human body is the best picture of the human soul' (*PI* p. 178)—is intended to be a response, but to which it inevitably runs the risk of being subjected in its turn. Its aim is to recall us to the difference between seeing the body as a meat machine and as the flesh and blood of expression.

A similarly literal or reductive interpretation of another genuine insight is also made manifest in our tendency to take the business with the manometer as revealing the proper functioning of psychological concepts. For, on the one hand, the ease with which we become preoccupied with that business might be thought to reflect our recognition that there must be a genuine point or purpose to the imagined entries of 'S' in my diary, because there is in general an internal relation between the meaningfulness of an utterance and the point or purpose of making it—an intimacy between the two primary aspects of this signature notion of 'use' (use as pattern of employment, use as sense or significance). After all, this perception is central to Wittgenstein's general vision of language, and hence to his particular treatment of words expressive of our inner state. We have already seen that articulating our inner life is not something we do out of a pure or sublimed commitment to recording the truth about our feelings simply and solely because it is the truth: if such self-ascription or self-description is a mode of self-acknowledgement, then it will be done for the reasons that human beings have for acknowledging things about themselves—perhaps most importantly, in order to seek acknowledgement of one's state, and so of oneself, from others, or in response to such (failures of) acknowledgement. This, I take it, is what Wittgenstein means to draw out in the following, later remarks:

...But isn't the beginning [of the language-game] the sensation—which I describe?—Perhaps this word "describe" tricks us here. I say "I describe my state of mind" and "I describe my room". You need to call to mind the differences between the language-games.

What we call "*descriptions*" are instruments for particular uses. Think of a machine-drawing, a cross-section, an elevation with measurements, which an engineer has before him. Thinking of a description as a word-picture of the facts has something misleading about it: one tends to think only of such pictures as hang on our walls: which seem simply to portray how a thing looks, what it is like. (These pictures are as it were idle.) (*PI* §§290–1)

But to say that a meaningful description has a point or purpose, rather than being utterly idle, is not to say that the only kind of point it can have is—let us say—merely utilitarian, pertaining to purely pragmatic or practical goals: as if purposeful descriptions must subserve the purposes of the engineer or the mechanic, rather than the painter or the poet (paintings can be allegorical as well as realistic—cf. *PI* §295). And in like manner, to say that meaningful self-descriptions have a point or purpose is not to say that, in the absence of a utilitarian purpose, they cannot have any meaning at all. But this seems to be precisely the assumption we are making about the resurrected diarist in §270. It is as if we regard his, and so our, capacity to express our inner state as somehow pointless or useless, quite without interest or significance, unless such expressions of ourselves might be made to do the kind of work done by a manometer. The sheer ease and completeness with which we lose ourselves in the apparently extensive ramifications of using 'S' as an indicator of blood pressure changes—treating that matter as if it alone determined the meaningfulness of the sign—strongly suggest that, for us, it is only if we make our diary keeping subserve a medical purpose, only if we (in effect) transform ourselves into human manometers, that we can think of our utterances as worth making, for others and even for ourselves.

If what made the sign 'S' meaningful—if what gave point or purpose to this utterance—were simply and solely its capacity to register a rise in blood pressure, that would amount to reducing an expressive utterance to the linguistic equivalent of a reddening of the cheeks. More precisely: our saying 'S' would be essentially analogous to a shifting of the levels of liquid in a manometer—essentially mechanical, an automatic, causal consequence of a physiological event. It is as if we are inclined to picture ourselves, *qua* beings capable of giving expression to our inner states, as no more than machines for one another's convenience—as if our utterances were merely one more way in which events within our bodies register outside it, as if the only interest we take in one another (and indeed, in ourselves) is a quasi-medical one, for which a human individual's articulation of her thoughts and feelings are of purely physiological significance. Words thereby appear as a convenient way of tracking otherwise invisible events whose nature and progress might permit certain kinds of prediction and interdiction, rather than as contributions to a relationship of mutual acknowledgement or denial.

One might say: the whole of that conversational domain—a domain of exchange, contestation, agreement and contradiction, the expression and acknowledgement of individuality and commonality, or its repression and refusal—appears as purely ornamental, the mere appearance of autonomy; the functional heart of language lies in its connection and its kinship with bodily mechanisms. Once again, then, the apparently ornamental, parenthetical, and belated image of the machine, seemingly appended to the paragraph purely as a dispensable convenience for its readers, turns out to be the key component of Wittgenstein's textual mechanism—a vehicle for diagnosing its readers, and allowing them to diagnose themselves, in essentially psychological terms (as possessed by, and giving expression to, certain fantasies in their modes of engagement with words), and so the embodiment of its inherently educative function. To change the image somewhat, although without entirely departing from the field of Wittgenstein's own imagery (cf. *PI* §§2 and 118), and without, I hope, suggesting its dispensability: the stone which the reader has (always already) rejected proves once again to be the cornerstone of Wittgenstein's philosophical enterprise.

Coda: Wittgenstein's Beetle (§293)

If I say of myself that it is only from my own case that I know what the word "pain" means—must I not say the same of other people too? And how can I generalize the *one* case so irresponsibly?

Now some tells me that *he* knows what pain is only from his own case!—Suppose everyone had a box with something in it: we call it a "beetle". No one can look into anyone else's box, and everyone says he knows what a beetle is only by looking at *his* beetle.—Here it would be quite possible for everyone to have something different in his box. One might even imagine such a thing constantly changing.—But suppose the word "beetle" had a use in these people's language?—If so it would not be used as the name of a thing. The thing in the box has no place in the language-game at all; not even as a *something*: for the box might even be empty.—No, one can 'divide through' by the thing in the box; it cancels out, whatever it is.

That is to say: if we construe the grammar of the expression of sensation on the model of 'object and designation' the object drops out of consideration as irrelevant. (*PI* §293)

Here is one way of reading this section. Wittgenstein is offering us a species of transcendental argument, which is designed to reveal a condition for the possibility of using a word as the name of an object (and so, one might think, a condition for the possibility of objecthood). If the word 'beetle' has a use in these people's language, then that use cannot be dependent upon its referring to the contents of their boxes, for it would be impossible for them to distinguish successful from unsuccessful reference—cases in which the term picks out its real referent from those in which it picks out another thing, or indeed nothing whatever. That distinction can be drawn only in the public realm, in which the presence or absence of the referent can at least in principle be checked by others. Since sensations are not public in this sense, sensation-terms cannot intelligibly be regarded as the names of objects, which amounts to the claim that sensations cannot intelligibly be regarded as a species of (inner) object. On this way of reading the section, it is hard to avoid thinking that we know exactly what it would be like if 'beetle' really did refer to the contents of these boxes, and that is why we know that it cannot be done. And consequently, it is all but inevitable that we will experience the transcendental condition we take ourselves to have unearthed as a limitation rather than a limit—that is, either as prohibiting us from doing something in particular, or as identifying a particular way things necessarily have to be.

Here is another way of reading this section. Wittgenstein is offering us a species of *reductio* argument, which aims to make patent the latent emptiness of the apparently intelligible idea that, if everyone had a box whose contents were accessible to themselves alone, the word 'beetle' might be used to refer to those contents (and thereby the latent emptiness of the analogous idea that 'pain' might designate an inner or private object known only to the person whose object it is). For by the conclusion of the 'argument', what we come to see is that the word 'something', pivotal to the content of the first two sentences articulating Wittgenstein's initial supposition, has not in fact been given a determinate meaning—at least, not one that will satisfy the interlocutor.

On this reading, the conclusion of Wittgenstein's reflections may at first seem strangely obtuse: for the possible emptiness of the boxes that it invokes as an apparently decisive blow to the original supposition does not look like a possibility that the supposition entails, or at least must allow for, but overlooks; it is, rather, one that it seems positively to deny. After all, doesn't Wittgenstein himself explicitly stipulate at the outset that each person's box has something in it, and not just something but some thing (*Ding*), as when he points out that each person might have a different thing, or a constantly changing thing, in his box? And isn't the tale his to tell; isn't his authorial status here absolute, so that what he says goes in this fictional universe?

If, however, on the basis of this stipulation that 'something' should in effect be read as 'some thing', he and we must acknowledge that the beetle might be different in each case, or constantly changing, then how can he or we exclude the further possibility of its absence? Is that not just as much a possibility of 'beetles' as their variety and mutability, if they really are a kind of object—a purely grammatical consequence of thinghood? Suppose we accept this. Even so, we might wonder how it could inflict any damage on the interlocutor's original claim about pain, which is meant to be the ultimate target of this analogical tale. For the possibility of someone's box being empty would surely be equivalent to that of a person who never experiences sensations of pain; but on the interlocutor's account, such a person would not be in a position to know what pain is, or consequently to know what 'pain' means. In other words, those with a use for 'beetle' surely are and must be those who have something in their boxes; the supposition of someone with an empty box would not reveal the self-subverting possibility of using 'beetle' even in the absence of an actual referent for it, but rather the unexciting possibility of someone having no use for this particular word.

To this, we might reply: but if each person knows what a beetle is only by looking in his own box, how is anyone to know that 'beetle' must refer to some actual thing, as opposed to whatever the box contains, which might perfectly well be nothing whatever? How, in other words, is anyone in a position to know, even in principle, that 'beetle' is the name of a thing? Not from others, for one cannot ever know to what others are referring when they refer to what is in their box as a 'beetle'; and not from ourselves, since all we can know is what is in our box. For those with empty boxes, therefore, 'beetle' is simply the name of nothing—in other words, not a name at all. Transposed to the case of pain, this means that those who never have sensations of pain would not thereby know that they had no use for the word 'pain'; since they cannot know whether others' use of 'pain' refers to anything or nothing, then anything at all that they might be feeling (including nothing at all) might justify their use of the word. But that simply means that here we cannot talk about correct or incorrect uses of the word; we cannot in fact talk about a meaningful word at all.

This is why Wittgenstein, at precisely the point at which the threat of emptiness is about to emerge from latency, asks us to suppose that the word 'beetle' has a use in these people's language. On the face of it, that is a peculiarly otiose supposition, since the story as a whole begins with him saying that we call whatever is in everyone's boxes a 'beetle', and continues by saying that these people make claims about their beetles (for example, that they know what beetles are by looking in their own box); so haven't we always already been supposing that the word has a use for all concerned? But precisely because of that, Wittgenstein's question is perfectly placed to invite us to ask ourselves whether we merely supposed that we were supposing this—whether we really understood him when he made that opening stipulation, or whether we merely thought that we did. For if it is true to say that 'The thing in the box has no place in the language-game at all; not even as a *something*', then who is in a position to say 'Suppose everyone had a box with something in it: we call it a "beetle" ', and what might they mean in so doing? If that use of 'something' is empty, then there is no 'it' for us to call a 'beetle', and hence no real grasp of what we are doing with that word.

In other words, we have implicitly been construing the whole of Wittgenstein's tale about beetles and boxes on the model of 'object and name'; but if the grammar of the word 'beetle' cannot meaningfully be construed along those lines, then neither can any part of the tale. From its very first sentence, then, this 'supposition' is empty, even if that emptiness becomes evident only belatedly; in that sense, we have no idea what we have been talking about in this section—of Wittgenstein's text, or of my text—even though we might feel that this is the conclusion that both texts have led us to, via a series of intelligibly linked claims.

How is this possible? But if it is not possible, how could any *reductio* argument deliver a genuine conclusion, by revealing the sheer nonsensicality of its apparent starting-point? And if *reductio* arguments really are legitimate means for gaining intellectual insight, then the position in which they leave us is surely no more uncomfortable than that offered to us by the *Tractatus*, with its concluding claim that a criterion for understanding its author is the realization that every elucidatory word of his must be recognized as simply nonsensical—as simply to be thrown away. Perhaps, when our concern is with the limits of sense, there is no other way of acknowledging them, and of inviting others to share that acknowledgement. And perhaps it is a criterion of properly understanding our difficulties here that we apprehend the latent nonsensicality of the previous sentence (with its simultaneous invocation and denial of another way, and hence its engendering of a sense of being methodologically limited, of there being something—some particular thing—that we cannot philosophically do).

No doubt, our false sense of understanding here was undergirded or encouraged by Wittgenstein's use of the word 'beetle' in articulating his putative analogy to a fantasy about 'pain' and pain—as opposed, say, to 'brillig', or '£$%^&', or '*'. For 'beetle' is a familiar word of everyday language, with a settled (even if sometimes unsettling) use in our form of life; hence it carries with it not only the general idea of an entity or object, but also a range of more specific connotations. I want to end by mentioning two, more or less figurative or (let us say) literary ones: the first internal or inner, the second external or outer.

Internally, 'beetle' recalls Wittgenstein's wriggling fly in §284: it suggests that, in order for the box people even to appear to merit comparison with people in pain, the contents of their boxes have to be not just substantial or objective, but animate.[1] It is as if,

---

[1] Severin Schroeder has recently suggested the following possible use for the word 'beetle' in these box people's language: 'Where we say "I am bored"', "You

in order to deny the body's capacity for expression—to effect its conversion to a mere receptacle, a hermetic container—we find ourselves having to put a living being, animate body and all, inside that box. But if the animation of the beetle is undeniable, why is that of the human body so hard to acknowledge?

The external literary connotation that seems unavoidable here (at least to me) is that of Gregor Samsa, the subject of one of literature's most famous metamorphoses (I am not sure whether it would help in eliciting the benefit of the doubt here to note that, at one point in his own private diaries, Samsa's creator speaks of his hopelessly inconsistent attempts to inhabit normal life as like 'the behaviour of a man who chases the wretched beggar from his door, and then when he's alone plays the benefactor by passing alms from his right hand to his left'.[2]) Gregor's story begins with what one might call the conjuring trick already having taken place:

As Gregor Samsa awoke one morning from uneasy dreams he found himself transformed in his bed into a gigantic insect. He was lying on his hard-armour-plated, back and when he lifted his head a little he could see his domelike brown belly divided into stiff arched segments on top of which the bed quilt could hardly keep in position and was about to slide off completely. His numerous legs, which were pitifully thin compared to the rest of his bulk, waved helplessly before his eyes.

What has happened to me? he thought. It was no dream. His room, a regular human bedroom, only rather too small, lay quiet between four familiar walls. Above the table on which a collection of cloth samples was unpacked and spread out—Samsa was a commercial traveller—hung the picture which he had recently cut out of an illustrated magazine and put into a pretty gilt frame. It showed a lady, with a fur cap on and a fur stole,

are cheerful" or "He is annoyed", those people use the expressions: "My beetle is boring me", "your beetle is pleasing you" and "His beetle is annoying him" (*Wittgenstein* [Cambridge: Polity Press, 2006], p 207]). One might say that my suggestion here is rather that, where we say 'I am bored' or 'He is annoyed', they use the expression 'My beetle is bored' and 'His beetle is annoyed', and so on.

[2] Quoted in Roberto Calasso, *K*, trans. G. Brock (London: Jonathan Cape, 2005), 150.

sitting upright and holding out to the spectator a huge fur muff into which the whole of her forearm had vanished![3]

Do we understand Kafka's imaginary tale, or is it another instance of literary nonsense, like Murdoch's Moy? It is hard to see why a philosopher's claims about the grammar of 'metamorphosis' or 'human being' or 'beetle' should have any more authority in this respect than our ability and willingness to follow Kafka's way of going on from his opening assertion.

Suppose, then, that we are willing to go on with him from this beginning. Does Gregor's condition and its vicissitudes amount to something better or worse than waking up and finding oneself turned to stone (*PI* §§283, 288)? Is accelerating confinement to (or absorption within) an insect's natural repertoire of expressions, desires, and capacities more or less attractive than utter unintelligibility in conjunction with complete inviolability? And is that question settled by the differences between life as a beetle and life as a stone, or rather by the specific ways in which specific others respond to these differences? Would Gregor swap his fate, at the hands of his family and their particular manifestations of shame, impatience, and self-interest, for that of a pebble or flint subject to Moy's particular cares and concerns?

We certainly begin by thinking of Gregor as having been trapped within an insect, rather as his words initially stand out from the background chittering of his voice, although that sense of confinement is certainly vitiated as his consciousness becomes increasingly immersed in insect preferences, needs, and vulnerabilities. But he never loses his consuming concern for his family's well-being; indeed, its inherently self-destructive tendency finds its ultimate expression in his willing embrace of death by starvation, understood by him as a way of ending the suffering that his new form of existence inflicts on his family (and understood by his readers

---

[3] 'The Metamorphosis', trans. W. and E. Muir, in F. Kafka, *The Complete Short Stories* (London: Vintage, 1999), 89; hereafter 'M'.

as the culmination of the suffering that their existence has inflicted on him—his new condition as an insect in this sense literalizing his fate as someone enslaved to the well-being of his relatives, his life having already been reduced to that of a drone utterly devoted to the flourishing of its hive or colony).

However, even if this slavishness is inseparable from who he is, it is not all that he is, even after his metamorphosis. For as his mother later explains to Gregor's employer, his job (and so his role as sole wage-earner) has not quite entirely consumed his existence.

The boy thinks about nothing but his work. It makes me almost cross the way he never goes out in the evenings; he's been here the last eight days and has stayed at home every single evening. He just sits there quietly at the table reading a newspaper or reading railway timetables. The only amusement he gets is doing fretwork. For instance, he spent two or three evenings cutting out a little picture-frame; you would be surprised to see how pretty it is; it's hanging in his room. (M 96)

Passing over the question of whether Gregor ever wonders whether what his paper says is true, or whether the departure times given for his trains are correct (cf. PI §265), this glancing remark returns us to the first object in his room to which he turns his gaze upon waking—the magazine picture whose pretty gilt frame we now learn is one that Gregor made himself. It is this picture alone that Gregor refuses to let his family remove from his room when they try to remodel it for his new condition: '[H]e was struck by the picture of the lady muffled in so much fur and quickly crawled up to it and pressed himself to the glass, which was a good surface to hold on to and comforted his hot belly. This picture at least, which was entirely hidden beneath him, was going to be removed by nobody' (M 118).

What might this picture mean to him, and so to us, that he is prepared to protect it with his already injured body, and so driven to find a foothold on a surface that might have seemed too smooth to yield it? If what matters is its frame or let us say form, then it represents his creative impulse—a trace of his ability to make his own individual mark on the world, at a time when he had hands with which to make such a mark. If what matters is what that frame frames, call it its content, then it represents first of all the unattained and unattainable possibility of love—itself marked by Gregor's later, sweet, and fleeting memories of 'a chambermaid in one of the rural hotels, . . . a cashier in a milliner's shop, whom he had wooed earnestly but too slowly' (M, 125). But the lady's fur is not just a symbol of sexuality; its sheer extravagance or excess, to the point at which she is muffled by it all, with her muff in particular threatening to swallow up the hands it is supposed to protect, suggests that part of its uncanny attractiveness for Gregor is its embodiment of animality, and in particular its embodying a presentiment of humanity (its hands uniquely equipped with opposable thumbs) being overwhelmed or taken over by animality.

Should we, then, regard the pretty frame he constructs for it as Gregor's way of trying to accommodate or control this dimly perceived threat in advance, to make it amenable to human handling (and so regard it as Kafka's way of reflecting upon the story in which it appears, as giving us a picture of its author attempting to employ the form of creative fiction to acknowledge and tame an uneasy, dreamlike fear of human animality)? If so, should we see Gregor's eventual fate as showing the ultimate failure of that attempt, and thus his ultimate dissolution into merely animate existence; or should we rather see his obdurate refusal to meet that fate except in the company of his framed picture as showing the ultimate failure of his new condition entirely to overwhelm his original, creative human individuality?

Either way, we should certainly not overlook the distinction encoded in the story's contrast between the lady's fur and the man's chitin—between a second skin (however hirsute) and an armour-plated, stiffly segmented exoskeleton; for just as we noted earlier the significance of the division within the material realm between the animate and the inanimate, so we are now encouraged to recall the division within the animate realm between animals and insects. Kafka is well aware that the fox or the bear has a dignity that the beetle or the cockroach sorely lack; as Gregor comes quickly to learn, the latter invite responses of repulsion and disgust rather than admiration and attraction. Sheathed in his insect armour, he is no longer able to elicit the pity that Wittgenstein takes to be a central form of the human conviction that another person is in pain (*PI* §287); his tale might even be said to mark the limits of our willingness to imagine humans taking non-human but animate form. For whilst we can go along with fairy-tales in which a prince has been turned into a frog, would we be willing to do so if told that he had been turned into one of the insects or flies that frogs eat? Gregor's family certainly find that they cannot maintain their conviction in his humanity in the absence of flesh and blood, not even the sister with whom he is especially intimate; the degree of his degradation in the hierarchy of being results in a lethal degradation in their responses to him.

What, by contrast, maintains our conviction as readers in Gregor's humanity is the fact that he never loses his narrative function as our point of view upon events, and so never loses his status as a being possessed of a perspective upon his own existence (at least, not until he no longer exists at all). In this sense, then, the form of Kafka's tale keeps faith with our sense of Gregor as surviving *within* rather than *as* the creature with which his family contends; and this inclines us towards a conception of the tale's protagonist as never entirely losing his humanity to his present condition. Consequently, we must in the end say that Kafka's beetle is the body, not its interior life; in Gregor's case, the soul is the insect body's prisoner, not (as with Wittgenstein's fly or beetle in a box) the insect itself.

So when Wittgenstein says that his beetle is cancelled out or divided through—as if it drops through the box's false bottom, the result of another conjuring trick (is this how the fly is meant to get out of the fly-bottle (*PI* §309)?)—should we see the result in terms of that figure's inner or its outer connotations—in terms of its internal or of its external literary life? Should we, in other words, cancel out the soul or the body? Perhaps we should rather aim to cancel our sense of the unbridgeable difference or division between them—that is, between the inner and outer ranges of reference of Wittgenstein's imagery, and so between the person and her expressive, flesh-and-blood embodiment.

Bibliography

Augustine, *Confessions*, trans. H. Chadwick (Oxford: Oxford University Press, 1991).

Baker, G. P., and Hacker, P. M. S., *Analytical Commentary on the* Philosophical Investigations, vols. 1 and 2 (Oxford: Blackwell, 1980 and 1986).

Calasso, R., *K*, trans. G. Brock (London: Jonathan Cape, 2005).

Cavell, S, 'Knowing and Acknowledging', in *Must We Mean What We Say?* (New York: Cambridge University Press, 1969).

——*Must We Mean What We Say?* (New York: Cambridge University Press, 1969).

—— *The Claim of Reason* (Oxford: Oxford University Press, 1979).

—— *The Senses of Walden: Expanded Edition* (San Francisco: North Point Press, 1981).

Conant, J., 'The Method of the *Tractatus*', in E. Reck (ed.), *From Frege to Wittgenstein* (Oxford: Oxford University Press, 2002).

—— 'Why Worry about the *Tractatus?*', in B. Stocker (ed.), *Post-Analytic Tractatus* (Aldershot: Ashgate, 2004).

—— and Diamond, C., 'On Reading the *Tractatus* Resolutely', in M. Kolbel and B. Weiss (eds.), *Wittgenstein's Lasting Significance* (London: Routledge, 2004).

Diamond, C., 'Rules: Looking in the Right Place', in D. Z. Phillips (ed.), *Wittgenstein: Attention to Particulars* (London: Macmillan, 1989).

Dummett, M., *Frege: Philosophy of Language*, 2nd edn. (London: Duckworth, 1983).

Finkelstein, D., *Expression and the Inner* (Cambridge, Mass.: Harvard University Press, 2003).

Hacker, P. M. S., *Analytical Commentary on the* Philosophical Investigations, vols. 3 and 4 (Oxford: Blackwell, 1990 and 1996).

Kafka, F., *The Complete Short Stories* (London: Vintage, 1999).

Malcolm, N., 'The Privacy of Experience', in A. Stroll (ed.), *Epistemology* (New York: Harper & Row, 1967).

Moore, A., 'Ineffability and Nonsense', *Proceedings of the Aristotelian Society*, supp. vol. 77, (2003), 169–93.

MULHALL, S., *On Being in the World: Wittgenstein and Heidegger on Seeing Aspects* (London: Routledge, 1990).

—— *Stanley Cavell: Philosophy's Recounting of the Ordinary* (Oxford: Oxford University Press, 1994).

—— *Inheritance and Originality: Wittgenstein, Heidegger, Kierkegaard* (Oxford: Oxford University Press, 2001).

MURDOCH, I., *The Green Knight* (London: Chatto & Windus, 1993).

SCARRY, E., *The Body in Pain* (Cambridge, Mass.: Harvard University Press, 1985).

SCHROEDER, S., *Wittgenstein* (Cambridge: Polity Press, 2006).

SULLIVAN, P., 'Ineffability and Nonsense', *Proceedings of the Aristotelian Society*, supp. vol. 77 (2003), 195–223.

WITTGENSTEIN, L., *Tractatus Logico-Philosophicus*, trans. O. K. Ogden (London: Routledge & Kegan Paul, 1922).

—— *Philosophical Investigations*, trans. G. E. M. Anscombe (Oxford: Blackwell, 1953; 2nd edn. 1958).

WOOD, M., 'Start Thinking', *London Review of Books*, 24/5 (7 March, 2002).

Index